Sta... Be up

NEVER GIVE UP

The Inspiring True Story About Brad Minns Who Overcame Deafness to Become A Champion at Tennis, Bodybuilding and Life

Brad Minns

Acknowledgements

Great books have always had an impact on my life and I am thankful to those who have spent the time to write books that have inspired me over the years to go for my dreams. The dream of writing this book came many years ago and I am grateful to those who have encouraged me not to give up on this dream.

Mom and Dad, thank you for being the greatest parents a kid could ever ask for, and for going many extra miles to give Jim and me such a great upbringing. Words alone can't express how grateful I am for everything you've done for me.

Brother Jim, thank you for all your love and support with which I would never have become the fighter you say I am.

To all my former coaches, teachers, neighbors, relatives and anyone else who has inspired me to become the best I can be on the court and off the court, thank you.

Larry J. Leech II, thank you for your patience over the past twelve months while this book was being written. I have learned a lot from you about writing a book.

Jimmy Vee, thank you for creating the awesome cover to this book. You do amazing work.

Linda Schiffer, thank you for all of your love and support throughout the years and always being there to lend support when I needed it the most.

Finally, to my beautiful wife, Ginny. You are the love of my life, best friend, and a gift from God. Thank you for believing in me and never giving up on my dream of writing this book. Without your expert proofreading and editing skills, I'd be in trouble. Every day I thank our Lord Jesus Christ for the blessings he has given us now and for eternal life.

Praise For Never Give Up

"I first heard Brad share his testimony at FCA's Night of Champions. Brad spoke with sincere conviction and authenticity about how God turned his life around. His life story will motivate and inspire you to overcome your obstacles and Never Give Up on your God given dreams!"

Pat Williams, Co-founder and Senior Vice President,
Orlando Magic, Author of
THE DIFFERENCE YOU MAKE

"In the athletic realm, being called "tough" is high praise. Some are called physically tough, others mentally tough....a few are called both. Then there are the Brad Minns' of the world. Not only physically and mentally tough, but emotionally, relationally and spiritually tough. When it comes to toughness, he is the total package. He has rebounded against great odds and excelled on and off the court. His is a story worth reading. You will be encouraged to hang tough amid your greatest challenges."

Kirk Cousins, Former Michigan State QB, Current
Member of the Washington Redskins

"Brad is an inspiration to me and many others and his story brings to light his faith, how he has handled challenges, and his uncompromising will to succeed in the activities that he pursues and in his life in general. Anyone can learn from his story."

Stan Smith, Former World No. 1 and 1987 Tennis Hall of Fame Inductee

"Never Give Up is relevant, insightful and extraordinarily inspiring! Brad Minns reminds us when we feel like giving up, look up to Christ and your strength will be renewed. If you desire to do more and be more read this book."

Roger Crawford, Best-Selling Author/ Motivational Speaker

"Brad Minns is a remarkable man whose testimony is tremendous! His life story is certain to touch your heart and strengthen your spirit! I highly recommend this book to everyone who is committed to seeing obstacles as opportunities. Brad's life challenges and inspires me to do great things for Jesus Christ!"

Del Wright, Vice President of Field Ministry, Southeast Central Region, Fellowship of Christian Athletes

"When it comes to determination, tenacity and grit, there are people who have it and there are people who don't... then there is Brad Minns. In these pages, you'll learn why "Never Give Up" is not just the title of this book but the personal mission statement of a man whose story and life are both educational and inspiring. Read it and discover the secret to getting anything in the World you want."

Jimmy Vee, Co-author of the best-selling book,
Gravitational Marketing: The Science of
Attracting Customers

"A successful bodybuilder and model, a gold-medal winning tennis pro ... all while being deaf. Some might glance at the life and times of Brad Minns and conclude that he was simply born with the ability to overcome and achieve. That would be missing the whole point. As you will find out in this book, Brad Minns' path to achievement and fulfillment is one that is accessible to every single one of us. It is about dreams and goals, discipline and attitude, and never, ever giving up. But these are merely the fruit. It is the God whom Brad serves that is the root ... and He wants to guide you down your own path to victory."

David Wheaton, author, radio host, tennis champion

CONTENTS

Foreword

Forty years ago when I first moved to California I had the opportunity to visit the Carmel Mission Basilica with my mother. In the museum my mom noticed a plaque with Father Junipera Sera's famous quote "Always Forward, Never Back," written more than 250 years ago. Father Sera was the founder of the California Mission system and brought Catholicism to the west coast of America in the 1700s. This quote best describes Father Sera's values that came from his deep prayer life and dauntless will to succeed. My mother bought me a replica of that plaque and told me to use these values when making my life choices and when choosing my friends. Years later when I told my mom about my lifelong friendship with Brad Minns she knew in her heart that I had made the right choice.

The road to success is littered with barriers, roadblocks and people simply getting in your way. Sometimes success means "never taking no for an answer." The first time I met Brad Minns was in Italy at the Italian National Deaf Tennis Championships in 1989. I was immediately drawn to him and impressed with his professionalism, his confidence and his will to win. It was my job as his tennis coach to watch out for him and help guide him to victory. During that tournament everything was stacked against us; the slow red clay, the rain delays, lack of transportation to the event, difficult scheduling and an unfriendly sentiment from the European teams toward our American team. But Brad never complained and went about the business of winning his matches. Ultimately the slow red clay and the Italians got to him and he did not win that event, but he began to make an impression on the world of deaf tennis.

In August of 1995 in Bradenton, Florida, at the Dresse Cup, the equivalent of the Davis Cup, Brad was on his home turf; the extreme sun and heat and hard courts. For one of his matches, I told him to be careful with Sydney, a 21-year-old English kid, who we knew from previous tournaments. Brad told me not to worry. I reminded him that Sydney was not a little kid anymore and

can be dangerous. Brad told me point blank, "I'll put him in the hospital." Brad did not say this in a mean-spirited way, just seemed to be telling a soon to be fact. Not more than thirty minutes into their match, there went Sydney in an ambulance off to the nearby hospital suffering from heat stroke. In the Florida sun, the European players just could not hold up and Brad simply bowled over any competitor that came his way. For the first time in the history of the Dresse Cup our USA team won the Gold medal, capping off the win with a doubles victory over Germany.

In Copenhagen, Denmark, at the 1997 Deaf Olympics, Brad and I worked hard on our game plans, practice sessions, nutrition and a rest program. Brad made it to the men's final, losing to the German Ronald Krieg in five long sets, and then came back later that day to win the gold medal in men's doubles in five hard sets against the German team, which included Krieg. Brad also won the Bronze medal in mixed doubles. He inspired other USA team members and we won sixty-percent of the total medals at those games. We also finally gained international recognition for the USA Team, as we were cheered on to victory by many other European countries.

More than 2,000 years ago, Aristotle wrote "We are what we repeatedly do. Excellence, therefore, is not an act but a habit." In the almost twenty-five years of my friendship with Brad, I have never seen him waiver in his quest for excellence in his life. Brad leads by example in his commitment to his wife Ginny and his family, his health and fitness, and his faith in God. He inspires his friends to follow his values and constantly keeps track on them to stay on task and he instinctively makes the right choices in life.

Stay Fit is Brad's trademark sign-off when he writes a letter or sends an email, and is a constant reminder to all to appreciate what God has given us and not to take anything for granted.

Brad has broken down the barriers that have been placed in front of him, he never takes no for an answer and always goes forward, never back.

Coach Rich Pèpe

Preface

"I first met Brad Minns at the Olympic Training Center in Colorado Springs in early summer, 1985. Chosen as one of four men and four women to represent the U.S. in the World Games for the Deaf, Brad was an affable, soft spoken young man, eager to begin our training in preparation for the Olympiad. Brad happily took on the rigors of the two-a-day practices and untold hours of off-court strategy sessions. He even supplemented the training with additional hours in the gym. What was not then known to me was his burning desire to win and incredible inner belief in his talent and preparation. In the Men's Singles final, competing for the Olympic gold medal, that steely determination would be put to the ultimate test. Behind two sets to love and 5-0 in the third, Brad's resolve stiffened. He fought back from what was certainly an insurmountable deficit to win a nearly four hour battle and take the Olympic Gold Medal. Brad's uncompromising will and determination to *Never Give Up* was an inspiration to me. His story will be an inspiration to you."

Michael LaPierre, Head Coach, United States Deaf Olympic Team, 1985, Los Angeles, CA

"It's hard to beat a person who never gives up."
Babe Ruth

Chapter 1 | World Champion

 I glanced up at the sky above the Pepperdine University tennis courts. The sun burned bright. I wiped a line of sweat from my brow. I glanced across the net at my opponent Jeff Osbourne, a teammate on the USA Deaf Olympic squad. He stood near the baseline, staring and probably wondering what was going on in my mind. Only one thought blasted through my mind: I'm not giving up.

If I had said those words aloud, anyone within earshot might have thought impossible. Whatever they may have said, I certainly would have replied I don't quit.

Quit. That word didn't exist in my vocabulary back then. Still doesn't today. So I took my spot on the baseline to serve. I wiped my brow again. Bounced the ball twice. Put it against my racquet. Tossed it in the air. Reached as far as I could. Hit it as hard as I could.

And thought, 'I can do this.'

Being down two sets to none and five games to none in the third in the Gold Medal match of the 15th World Games for the Deaf isn't the ideal situation for a tennis player. But that's where I found myself that warm

Saturday afternoon in July 1985. Up to this point, Osbourne, the defending champion, had played a near-perfect match. I fought him off the best I could, but he was more determined than I had ever seen him. We first met during the trials held at *Gallaudet University* near Washington, D.C. I beat him in the trials to earn my spot on the team. Then we trained together for six weeks in Colorado Springs, so I'm sure he felt he had something to prove in this match. He also was the defending champion.

And he played like it.

The scoreboard showed 4-6, 5-7, and 0-5 in Osbourne's favor, in the best three of five sets. In the sixth game of the third set, I decided I needed to take control of the match. At one point Osbourne missed a long volley by about six to eight feet. I don't recall that particular shot. Our coach Michael LaPierre later said he thought that was the turning point. I remember various other times in the match that momentum was turning in my favor.

In that third set, I could have settled for winning a few more games, maybe even a set, but I was determined to fight back. All the way back—despite the insurmountable lead Osbourne had built.

So the long trek back started. One point. One game. One set at a time.

To get some encouragement during the changeovers, I gazed over to the stands, where my coach and only a handful of spectators sat. Just a few minutes earlier there weren't many seats available because so many people came out to watch. Since the match was a blowout up to that point, many disappointed fans headed for the exits. Who could blame them? I looked over to my coach for some kind of mental boost. Since Osbourne and I were both on the USA team, Coach LaPierre was reluctant to favor one of us over the other.

I was alone with so many thoughts. Every couple of points I'd look up to see if my family had arrived yet. Nothing. Later I had discovered their plane was delayed. It wouldn't have been any fun for them to watch me losing so handedly, yet I hoped they would be there.

My efforts were paying off as I worked my way back and won the next two sets. The score was tied at two sets apiece with the fifth set just beginning. Word spread throughout the Olympic grounds that there was a comeback in the making on our court. Spectators who had left earlier began returning to the stands. Fans were cheering for their favorite player to win the match. What a difference a few hours make. One minute I was on the brink of defeat and losing with no support. Now here I was, closing in on victory with everyone cheering me on with their arms raised in the air and hands waving back and forth. This I learned is how the deaf cheer.

The fifth and final set was pretty close. With Osbourne's stamina quickly going downhill, I decided to come to the net more since he started staying back at the baseline. All those hours spent in the gym started paying off. I could sense him becoming physically and mentally tired after he had been so close to winning his second consecutive championship in the third set. Even though he was physically exhausted, he still fought back hard and wouldn't surrender. After holding serve to make it 5-4 in my favor, I found myself sitting at the changeover amazed at what had just taken place. I still had one more game to win to claim the gold medal.

Osbourne was showing obvious signs of disgust and frustration having lost such a commanding lead. The last game turned out to be the most difficult. He needed to hold serve to stay in the match, while my objective was to break his serve. We battled back and forth. Point after point. The score was deuce, then my advantage. After surviving through several deuce/add exchanges, I needed only one point to win the biggest match and comeback of my tennis career up to that point.

My thoughts began to jump around like a pin ball

machine, wandering a little bit and I had a hard time focusing. I fought to stay focused on the winning thoughts.

I reminded myself once again what I had done

earlier, put one foot in front of the other, and played one point at a time. I whispered a prayer asking God for help. I glanced to see if Mom, Dad and my cousin Mark had arrived. I looked to the stands for support. Then it was back to business.

Osbourne served to my backhand. My heart raced as I stepped in to strike the ball using my two-handed backhand. Seeing the ball clear the net was a relief. Now it was Osbourne's turn. He hit the ball back and charged the net to put pressure on me. Unfazed, I smacked it right back at him. Then following a quick split-step, Osbourne volleyed and netted the ball.

After almost five hours of grueling tennis, I had finally won the match. I thrust my arms into the air. I had done it. I had come back from an unbelievable deficit. I had won the fifth set, 6-4, to claim the gold medal. I had won my first Deaf Olympic Tennis Championship and became the best deaf tennis player in the world.

Some may not have believed what they just saw. But the scoreboard didn't lie: 4-6, 5-7, 7-6, 6-3, 6-4 in my favor, then just a 20-year-old sophomore at the University of Toledo.

A few moments later, the medal ceremony was held using the format people are familiar with in the regular Olympics. When it was my turn, I bent low for the official to place the gold medal around my neck. While the big USA flag was being raised behind me, I held a smaller USA flag high and smiled. There was so much emotion. I had a strong feeling of patriotism seeing my country's colors lifted high. We all knew we were playing for our country, but in that moment, when you stand there, the victory won, you realize it's not about you. I didn't recognize the true meaning of selflessness until years later. But that day on the court, I got a glimpse of having won something bigger than me. I took a moment to shake hands with Osbourne, someone whom I admired and respected, and the bronze medalist, a young man from Italy.

After the ceremony was over, the gold medal was still around my neck when my family finally arrived. They noticed the medal and I enthusiastically explained how I had won a few moments earlier. My mother was glad they missed the match because it would have been too emotional for her to watch. They were all excited, happy, and relieved that I won.

Twenty years later, I gave that medal to a man Bill Austin, Founder and CEO of Starkey Hearing Technologies. His company sponsored our team during the games and fitted the deaf athletes from all over the world with hearing aids. Austin did a lot for us, and I wanted to repay him. I'll share more about that event in the chapter titled "Giving Back."

Now, here I was ... thousands of miles away from my hometown in Ohio ... a twenty-year-old sophomore at the University of Toledo ... and a world champion.

The next day the Orange County Register quoted me as saying, "I never came back from that far in my life. ...What a comeback."

That wasn't my only comeback while in Los Angeles. I faced three other obstacles before meeting Osbourne in the medal match. I arrived as the No. 1 seed in the tournament after ripping through opponents, including Osbourne, in the qualifying events. Soon after arriving in the City of Angels, two events knocked me from my lofty perch. The first was a jaywalking ticket, something unheard of in my hometown of Toledo, Ohio. A few days later, the Italian coach challenged my seeding with a formal protest. The coach claimed I didn't deserve the top seeding, or any seeding for that matter, because I'd never competed in the World Games for the Deaf or the Dresse Cup—deaf tennis' equivalent of the Davis Cup. By a 6-4 vote of the coaches, I lost my seeding and was forced to play Italy's top player, Pier Paolo Ricci-Bitti in the first match. I won that match easily, thanks to something Mike said to me prior to the start of the tournament. He said, "Brad, there is nobody in the world that can embarrass you on the tennis court."

He must have thought highly of my game to say that because I hung on to those words throughout my college tennis career and many other times I have played some very tough matches.

My setbacks weren't over, though. I had one more hurdle to clear. Following my victory over Spain's Vincent Ortola, I needed to answer some questions from a reporter so I put in my hearing aids. Spain's coach thought I had played the match with my hearing aids, which is forbidden by the Deaf Tennis Association. The Spanish coach saw the hearing aids in my ears and went ballistic, ranting and raving about this and that in Spanish. His protest lasted more than two hours.

After the ruling in my favor, I was able to concentrate on the next matches and eventually made it to the Gold Medal match against Osbourne, who won his title four years prior during the games in Berlin, West Germany. So, on July 13, 1985, Osbourne, who was five years older, and I stepped onto the court to determine who would be the best deaf singles tennis player in the world. Osbourne, possibly stung by my sudden emergence as a major player, got off to a great start.

"Through the first two and a half sets I think Osbourne played a perfect match," recalls Mike LaPierre, coach of the U.S. team. "Brad didn't play poorly. He made some nice shots, but Jeff didn't make mistakes."

When Osbourne missed that shot in the third, LaPierre said it looked "like someone had punched (Jeff) in the gut."

There were a number of shots thrown that were like gut punches throughout the match, especially in the third when I was on the ropes and Osbourne had more match points than I can remember. Every one of those match points that Osbourne lost must have felt like gut punches to him but a burst of relief for me. Each time I fought off a match point it gave me renewed hope and optimism to keep pressing forward.

I won my Gold Medal that day because of hard work and determination, something my teammates witnessed during preparation at the USA Olympic Training Center (OTC) and U.S. Air Force Academy, both in Colorado Springs, Colorado. I loved those "great training facilities," particularly the gym at the OTC. As someone who loves weight training, it was a match made in heaven. After working out in the gym, there was an incredible buffet of food. All fit for a king! In my mind I was thinking ahead to the games. I had high expectations and didn't want to waste time. After hours of practice on the tennis courts, I headed straight for the gym or a long run while my teammates went off to do what they wanted.

My focus was to win. And to me, that meant spending a lot of time in the gym. Back then coaches and trainers discouraged us from lifting weights. They felt big muscles would hinder our tennis game. Nowadays, it's recommended for tennis players to train with weights and spend time off-court training. Winning and being successful by worldly standards was my motivation.

Despite running and lifting, I still got to spend plenty of time with my USA teammates. I really enjoyed being around everyone, laughing and having a good time. We all got along well and had so much fun in spite of our communication challenges, me being an oral communicator and most of my teammates using sign language. I did sneak away regularly to get my workouts in, but I remember all the off-court fun we had. They even gave me the sign language name of brat because of how much I joked around and played practical jokes.

I recall this one prank where some of the guys decided to play a joke on the girls' team while they slept. The deaf rely on flashing lights for a fire alarm. My Dad and I learned this at tryouts while we were sleeping. In the middle of the night the lights started flashing on and off. My Dad and I didn't know what was going on except that everyone was running for the exits. So we ran out the door and followed them. Later we learned it was a fire drill. Remembering that experience, my teammates and I took the flash from a camera and put it in the girls' dorm room. We turned it on and ran out while the camera started flashing. We had a great laugh watching all the girls run out of their room in their pajamas.

Another time us guys took a bucket of water and placed on top of a door to soak the next unsuspecting female. When the prank worked to perfection we got a great laugh. Every day was like that. Just fun and laughs all the time.

Well, not all the time. We had to get serious when we practiced. LaPierre pushed us hard through well-organized practices. He was slow to speak and a good listener. I appreciate the time we spent together, talking not only about tennis but about life as well.

I first found out about the World Games for the Deaf, which were later changed to the Deaflympics, one day while preparing to practice at the Toledo Tennis Club, a local hangout for those who loved tennis. My college coach Bob Longley approached me with a newspaper clipping about the size of a large postage stamp. I skimmed through the one paragraph announcement. I couldn't believe my luck. I had never heard of the games for other deaf tennis players like me. I don't remember much about what happened at practice that day. All I wanted to do was to get home to tell my parents about this exciting opportunity. Mom, Dad and my brother Jim were just as excited as me and gave me the thumbs up to pursue.

Dad accompanied me to the tryouts at Gallaudet University. This was our first experience in the deaf culture. Because of my parents' determination for me to function in a hearing world, I didn't learn to sign, which proved a hindrance on this trip. When we arrived at the campus we needed to ask for directions. The gentleman we asked looked confused until we realized he couldn't understand us. So I wrote down the location and in simple sign language he led us to the dorm location where we were to stay. Dad and I laughed because our signing skills needed a lot of work. Actually, they still do. I prefer to talk and read lips. The "good morning" sign, which is similar to the "up yours" sign quickly became our favorite, our little inside joke. So we'd give each other the "good morning" sign all the time in good fun.

That tryout started my first journey into deaf tennis. By the time I headed to Los Angeles, I was aware of my opportunity to do something huge, something far beyond what I imagined when I first picked up a racquet at age six. The first time I tried tennis, I felt like a failure. It was difficult for me to learn and I didn't want to continue with my  lessons. However, my parents persisted and I eventually grew to love the game.

I said earlier in this chapter, my time in Los Angeles didn't start well. Roadblocks and obstacles could have discouraged me and caused me to give up. Champions will tell you, though, it's not about the obstacles, everyone encounters them, but rather it's about overcoming the obstacles in life and on the tennis court. That's a common trait in winners, overcoming and finishing strong.

The future looked bright. At twenty years old I had more mountains to climb. I didn't know which ones at the time. Sitting on my laurels was—and to this day still isn't—my style.

And unbeknownst to me, my greatest victory was still ten years away.

"Although the world is full of suffering,
it is also full of the overcoming of it."
Helen Keller

Chapter 2 | Growing Up

I was raised, along with my brother Jim, in Sylvania, Ohio, a town of about 20,000 near the Michigan line and home to the Jamie Farr (of M*A*S*H fame) LPGA Classic. A great place to raise kids, I loved spending time at the pool in the summers, eating hot dogs, laying in the grass and looking up into the clear blue skies without a care in the world.

On weekends in the summer, my friends and I played baseball downtown at Memorial Field. I enjoyed putting on my clean, pressed uniform and riding my bike to the games. If we won coach treated the team to ice cream at Custard's Last Stand. Baseball was my favorite sport growing up and I was a pretty good second baseman on the "A" team. My coach alerted the umpires of my hearing loss. After stepping inside the batter's box, the umpire gave me the count with his hands.

Growing up without hearing was tough in many ways. A child not only must learn to function in a hearing world either with sign language or reading lips, but learn to deal with the difficulties of being teased by children who could hear. Schoolmates have a knack for making life tough on another who isn't like them. I was no exception.

I was three years old when my family discovered I lost my hearing. I don't remember the exact details, but know I became ill with a high fever. The fever lasted several days. Imagine my disbelief when I recovered only to awaken in complete silence. I'd never hear another Saturday morning cartoon, my brother call my name, or my parents offer me a word of encouragement or support.

What I do remember is the day the Millers, a husband and wife team, came to the house in 1969 to show us the new technology that promised the opportunity for a person like me the ability to hear. At first I was excited about the chance to hear again, but that ended when I saw the contraption I needed to wear.

Mr. Miller was tall with a deep voice and mustache. He also smelled like tobacco. Strange as it may sound, I enjoyed the pipe smoke smell. It reminded me of my Grandpa Minns. Grandpa Minns, thanks to grandma, always had fresh tobacco. I can still remember the room we all sat in while we visited them on Gallatin Road in Ottawa Hills, a suburb of Toledo not far from where my brother and I grew up. So I felt comfortable around Mr. Miller.

After testing my ears with a special tester, a box-like computer, one of the Millers placed headphones over my ears, the big clunky kind you see pilots wear in the old black and white war movies. With the headphones on, I raised the corresponding hand when I heard a beep in one of my ears. When the Millers finished, they huddled with Mom and Dad to discuss which aid would help me to hear again.

I wasn't happy with the decision. I needed to wear a bib-like piece that reminded me of a woman's bra. I think I screamed "no" as loud I could and probably added, "I don't want to wear that bra."

But I had no choice. If I wanted to hear, I had to wear the hideous device. Inside the bra a compartment held the hearing aid transistor, which was about the size of a modern day cell phone. Despite the size, the worst part was the protruding wires that ran up through my shirt and connected to the hearing aids. I loved the television show *My Favorite Martian* and at times I felt like one of the characters with all the wires and molds, and bibs and boxes. I wondered how I'd muster up the courage to leave the house and face people.

But I did. When the Millers finished hooking me up to the device, I did what all little boys wanted most—went outside and played. I loved being outside as a kid. Later I became a couch potato, but at this age, I wanted to be outside. I enjoyed playing in the yard with friends. That day when I left the house, I remember hearing something I'd never heard before. I didn't have to focus on the sound. It drifted into my new hearing aids. I got chills. I could hear the wind.

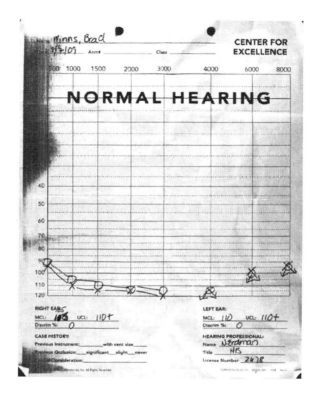

Excited, I went looking for other sounds and to discover what my hearing aids could pick up. With my new hearing aids I was now able to hear the sounds of cars, trucks, planes and construction when outside. Also, I loved the sound of the voices of my family members. I especially enjoyed the laughter when Dad told a story or joke. Later, I learned to read their lips and I was able to distinguish each person's voice. With my type of hearing loss I am better able to understand the lower pitch voices than the high ones.

Not only was I able to hear more sounds, I attracted a lot of attention from curious onlookers. I soon became known as the little guy from Sylvania with the hearing aids.

Despite the unwanted attention I managed to survive nursery school, a small country school called Little Meadows near where we lived. I think I cried my first day when my mom dropped me off but she'll probably tell you I was a brave little guy. What child doesn't cry when dropped off their first day of school? So, at least for a day, I fit in with the rest of the kids. My favorite part of the day soon became the time Mom picked me up. Because each day was a struggle, going home to the comfort of familiar surroundings and all the love I wanted was the highlight of my day.

Mom and Dad wanted to ensure I could read lips and communicate orally so later in life I would excel in the hearing world. They felt it was better for me to not learn sign language. Instead of attending a special school for the deaf, I was enrolled in a "hearing" school. I began seeing a speech therapist while at Little Meadows Nursery School and continued through my early years of Highland Elementary School. Each day, Mom picked me up from school. We got a quick bite at Dutch Pantry, my favorite place to eat onion rings, before heading to downtown Toledo to see a speech therapist. I didn't enjoy seeing the therapist. At times, it felt like torture. I wore headphones and took tests with different sounds, watched my teacher's lips and then tried to say words and sentences that were hard to pronounce. The therapist also insisted I drink my milk, which I hated. After a while, my pronunciation improved and I could distinguish the difference in various sounds. Despite all the work with the therapist, I learned the most at home, thanks to the love and sacrifice of mom, dad, and brother Jim.

When finished at the therapist's office, we headed home where I played kickball, capture the flag, basketball,

interception and all kinds of fun games with my brother and the neighborhood kids. When Dad arrived home from work at 5:30, he'd put on his shorts and come out to play with us. Dad always made time for us kids and often coached our baseball and basketball teams. When Mom called us in for dinner, we were done playing for the night. After dinner, we focused on homework. Mom sat with me to make sure I was staying on top of my schoolwork. Honestly, I don't know how she kept up with everything. She was patient with me when we went over everything we did in every class. This sometimes took a lot of time. But we weren't done. She also made me read out loud and corrected the words I struggled with. Even today I may mispronounce certain words and need someone to correct me.

My next school was Highland Elementary. New kids, new teachers, new environment. A scary time, for sure. In what became a habit, when I started a new school my mom and dad made sure the teachers knew about my hearing impairment. I needed to sit in the front row, which I didn't mind. Not only did I get to sit close enough to read my teacher's lips, I got to sit close enough to see the big clock on the wall. I loved those big school clocks with the second hand large enough to watch the seconds tick by. Now a tad older, I was a little more self-conscious about what the wires looked like dangling from my ears. And what other people thought of them. Some kids wanted to know what they were for, others tried to yank them out. Each day was a challenge and each day I couldn't wait to get home.

I didn't enjoy music class and struggled through it in elementary school. We had to sing, read musical notes, and listen to music and songs I couldn't understand. One day we played a game similar to Pictionary. We were paired off and our partner was to write a word on a card for the other to act out the word for the rest of the class to guess. My partner wrote the word guitar. To everyone else in class, that was a simple word. For me, I had no idea what a guitar was. I thought guitar sounds like katar with a "K."

When the "G" came first I had no idea what it was. My partner took me into the hallway to explain it. He went on and on, imitating playing a guitar, often jumping up and down with a look on his face that I should understand his actions. After a few moments, I shrugged and said forget it. I am happy now to say I know the difference between a guitar and a katar.

Another time, when I was in the fifth grade, the teacher discussed careers with the class. She talked about various jobs we could aspire to, like doctor, fireman, athlete, beauty contest winner, baker, to name a few. She then lined up the boxes—each labeled with a career choice—at the front of the room. After she divided us into small groups we were instructed to write our name on a piece of paper and place it in one of the boxes. I misunderstood the instructions so I put my name in all the boxes. When she drew the names for each box, guess who won the beauty contest? The class enjoyed a great laugh at my expense.

I challenged myself at school as much as possible. I pushed myself to finish first when taking a math test and to make perfect letters in writing class. In grade school, I won a spelling bee. I also won a book mark contest for creating the best bookmarker. Mine said: To be a leader, be a reader. I won a ribbon and have loved receiving awards for things like that because it gave me the sense of accomplishment. In Cub Scouts, I made sure I finished my assignments before the others so I would have the most beads on my shirt. This also boosted my sense of worth.

To improve or restore my hearing, my parents decided to try acupuncture. This technique was new in the U.S. and we took our first trip to Washington, D.C., for treatment in 1974. I wasn't thrilled with the idea of someone sticking needles in my head. It didn't matter to me at the time that one million Chinese believed in the technique.

My first visit to the acupuncture center was scary. I saw people walking around the office with needles protruding out of their heads. I remember  thinking that I didn't want to go in there. I didn't want someone sticking me with a bunch of needles. However, I did muster up the courage to lie on the table. My heart raced while I waited for the doctor.

After he explained the procedure to Mom and me, he pushed a number of needles into the back of my ear. I screamed, loud enough that Jim left because he couldn't take seeing his little brother in pain. The needles remained in my ears for a little while. When the doctor removed them, the room smelled of marijuana when a soothing device was heated up to rub behind my ear. The device brought relief but I couldn't stand the smell.

I was treated every day for a week, which allowed us to stay during the Fourth of July celebration. We enjoyed the most incredible fireworks display from the hotel window overlooking our nation's capital.

When the treatments ended, tests showed I did have some improvement in my hearing. I received treatment like this for three years. I dreaded those trips but loved the sightseeing in Washington, D.C.

From elementary school, I advanced to McCord Junior High which was a bit farther away from home than my first two schools. This meant I rode a school bus for the first time. While most kids hurried to sit in the back, I usually settled into a seat near the front. Sitting here allowed me to enter and exit quickly, which was important to me at the time. Kids in the back were noisy, rowdy and sometimes mean.

During junior high I began wearing more powerful and much smaller hearing aids that fit behind my ears. I liked these better because they didn't have wires that came up out of my shirt. When I grew my hair long enough you hardly noticed them, except when I had to change batteries. When the new aids got quiet, I knew it was time to change batteries. Because of this, I tried to change the batteries during the break between classes. However, sometimes I requested a bathroom pass in order to change my batteries while no one looked on.

Every now and then I had to deal with kids who belittled my hearing impairment by covering their mouths. I guess it gave them some kind of ego boost. I didn't let it bother me too much, but deep down it was tough. Like most kids that age I was self-conscious. I worried about my hearing aids falling out during tumbling and gymnastic type moves in gym class or getting my hearing aids wet from running around and sweating. Moisture caused them to make various noises that made it difficult to hear.

Like in elementary school, I couldn't wait for the school day to end so I could get home to my safe surroundings and family support. I especially loved bedtime. I still remember all the blankets and pillows on my bed. The walls of my sky blue room were covered with posters of my favorite athletes. My very own desk sat against one wall. The book shelves were lined with Hardy Boys books. My parents' room was across the hall from mine. Many times before bed, Dad told the best bedtime stories and made the coolest special effects sounds, and faces to make the story seem lifelike. A record player sat next to my bed. I owned most of Olivia Newton-John's records, as well as some Beach Boys records. Hearing the words of the songs was tough for me so Jim wrote out the words for each song and lip synced so I would learn each word. This allowed me to follow along and enjoy the music a little bit more. Mom would turn off my record player when she saw I was asleep.

Each morning I'd peek out of the corner of my eye, hoping I still had more time in bed. Or I would look out the window and hope it had snowed enough the previous night to force a delay or cancellation of school.

It's not that I didn't enjoy school. I did for the most part. I received average grades, but I grew tired of being teased by the other kids and worrying about making a fool of myself in class. Every day was a new challenge. Without the love and support of my family, I would have never made it through junior high.

I entered Sylvania Northview High School, home of the Wildcats, in 1980. Today almost 1,500 students attend the school. Back then was about the same. The night before my first day I couldn't sleep because of butterflies in my stomach. Again, new students, new teachers, but also new situations: girls.

Northview High school presented a whole new opportunity to grow stronger as a person because of many new challenges, particularly in the classroom. The work was tougher. Again I sat in the front row, but many times the teachers forgot about my hearing loss and turned their backs to the class while giving us instructions. Math was especially hard, so my parents hired a well-known math tutor, Sue Bissonette. Despite their efforts, this subject was a challenge for me.

During my freshman year, my brother Jim was a senior. He was a star athlete, one of the top students, a member of the debate team, and took advanced classes. I felt encouraged by his presence and was a proud little brother when we passed each other in the hall.

I was an undersized freshman, which caused me a lot of grief that year. One time while playing soccer in gym class, I kicked the ball as hard as I could … right into the face of a girl. Instead of crying, she charged me like a lion. I escaped harm the day, but because I was an easy target, I endured a lot of teasing from my classmates. I didn't have the firepower to fight back. That changed when I started lifting weights.

In senior high, lunchtime was a challenge for me. The noise in the cafeteria made it difficult to filter out conversations in large groups, so I tried to sit in smaller groups. Many times I retreated to the library, a place where I met up with several of my friends to study. In the library we shared a good laugh frequently and I'm thankful our librarian didn't kick us out for making noise.

Like most boys in high school, girls became an interest. In my bedroom, posters of athletes were replaced with beautiful iconic women, such as Cheryl Tiegs, Farrah Fawcett, and Olivia Newton-John. At school, several girls took notice despite my hearing challenge, but the thought of going out on dates made me very nervous. I was insecure about how a girl might respond if I couldn't hear her in the dark or if my hearing aids started beeping when I kissed her.

My Friday nights where usually spent on the sofa waiting for the television lineup of *Fantasy Island* and *The Love Boat*, two of my favorite shows at the time. On the bright side, staying at home with my parents kept me from drinking, smoking, and taking drugs.

When I did get up the nerve to ask a girl on a date, I almost wrecked the car a few times. Not from trying to impress the girl, but because I turned to look at her when she spoke. One time I swerved all over the road and hit about a half dozen speed bumps. I apologized profusely to my now scared-out-of-her-mind date. Another time a police officer, thinking I was a drunk driver, stopped me. When I explained my situation he let me off with a warning.

Getting together with immediate family members was always, and still is, important. We spent many summer hours on Grandma's patio drinking fresh squeezed lemonade and enjoying homemade sugar cookies. During Thanksgiving holidays, Dad took my brother, some cousins and me muskrat trapping at a local creek. We'd go out the day before to set our traps. Thanksgiving morning we rose early to see what we caught. We usually found three or more muskrats in our traps. We took our bounty home and skinned it. Grandma mixed the meat with cream of mushroom soup for one of her delicious treats.

Dad also took my brother and me bird or small game hunting not far from where we lived. I admired not only my dad's work ethic, but also his expert hunting,  trapping, and fishing skills. One of my favorite stories about Dad and me was the summer we drove to the French River, near the top of Canada, where Dad knew some of the native Indians. He befriended them years before when he removed a fishing hook from one of the guides. He used the skills acquired during his service as a corpsman in the Korean War to remove the hook. The Indian family often asked Dad to come back for a visit. During our trip, Dad and I did quite a bit of fishing.

Our usual routine after catching them was to dock the boat, start a camp fire and eat the fresh fish, along with potatoes, cooked with lard and salt. Everything tastes better out in the open air, especially in a beautiful place. After eating we'd rest along the river bank and admire the surroundings of lakes, hills and trees.

Later, we decided to hunt from the boat. Being an inexperienced hunter, I pointed to some birds flying by and started to ask whether I was allowed to shoot them. My dad, being the quick decision maker in the family, took out his gun and, before I could finish my sentence, got off two quick shots to bring down the birds. Wanting to prove myself as a coming-of-age hunter, I asked Roley, the Indian guide, and Dad to drop me off on a secluded island in the middle of nowhere. I placed decoys in the pond to attract ducks. Because I wore bright blue jeans I thought I'd need to camouflage myself. I gathered branches and sticks to cover up and waited patiently for game birds to fly overhead. Some time had passed before a large flock of birds swooped down towards the decoys. I attempted to bust free from the thick camouflage, only to discover I was stuck under the heavy weight of the branches and couldn't get out in time to shoot the birds. Instead of game birds, we enjoyed leftovers for dinner, thanks to Roley's wife.

Every Christmas Eve the Minns family gathered at Aunt Janet's where everyone brought their favorite dish and spent time reconnecting. I didn't know it when I was young, but my dad dressed up as Santa Claus. He'd have the little kids sit on his knee and share their favorite

Christmas songs with the family. Then from his sack he gave them a candy cane filled with M&Ms. Kids love Dad and he connects well with young children, as well as people from all walks of life. I learned a lot by watching my dad relate to people.

I received a lot of love and encouragement from my family. Without it, I never could have dealt with the issues during elementary, junior high, and high school. I believe everyone has a rock in their life. Growing up, my family was that rock for me. Later, I learned of another rock on which to stand. During this time, it was my family—my

dad and mom, and, of course, my brother Jim.

Growing up in that kind of environment rubs off on you. At first, I wanted to stay in the comfort zone of being at home, but eventually wanted to strive and do more. And I did, thanks to their encouragement.

They laid the groundwork for shaping me into who I am today.

"If you don't practice you don't deserve to win."
Andre Agassi

Chapter 3 | Tennis

Mom introduced me to the game of tennis when I was five. She thought tennis would be an opportunity for me to learn the sport she loved to watch and play. Because of my hearing impairment, she hoped tennis would help me learn how to focus, and to communicate with other kids my age.

I couldn't play contact sports, such as football and ice hockey, because both require wearing a helmet. I couldn't because of my hearing aids. To make matters worse, whenever I got hit in the head by a ball, my ears rang and I couldn't hear anything again until the ringing stopped. Because of the ringing I'd have to stay home from school until I could hear again. I loved baseball more than tennis. I preferred the simplicity of hitting a baseball with a heavy aluminum bat as hard as I could. I also loved the camaraderie of being on a baseball team. If I got on base, my teammates gave me high-fives and patted me on the back. If we won the game we got free ice cream, compliments of the coach, which oftentimes was my dad. By the time I reached high school, I dropped all other sports to focus on tennis.

Tennis then became my sport. I struggled right from the beginning. Our lessons were held in Sylvania on five adjacent courts. Our instructor, Barb, lined us up along the baselines of each court. I could read her lips if she was near and facing me. When she walked away I learned to watch the other kids to see what she wanted us to do. At times, I felt like I lived in my own little world and wanted to stay at home.

It seemed the other kids had a pretty easy time picking up the game. I was uncoordinated and I couldn't get the ball over the net. This frustrated me. My mom wanted this to be a confidence booster, but it was the opposite for me. After a while I didn't want to play anymore. Coach Barb explained to my mom that even if it didn't look like it at the time, she thought I was one of the most natural tennis players she'd ever seen. This encouraged my mom to keep me in the game and not allow me to give up.

I struggled to properly hit the ball and I disliked the running needed to get into playing shape. Especially when Coach Barb and her assistant made us run in the heat of the day. I can't emphasize enough how much I disliked running in the heat.

Tennis is a difficult sport to learn. A person has to master a number of different shots: forehand, backhand, top spin, back spin, kick serves, slice serves, volleys, lobs, etc.

It takes a lot of practice to master the muscle memory of each.

Despite my constant complaining, my family encouraged me to stick with it. They didn't allow me to feel sorry for myself. Mom often said, "Are you a man or a mouse? You have to get up and face the challenges or do you want to stay home and be afraid?" This was mom's way of showing me tough love. And I needed it.

I also needed a lot of practice to improve my game. I remember times when Dad got up early in the morning to toss me balls to hit. Then we'd eat breakfast and he'd go to work and I'd go to school. I'm blessed to have a family that believed in me.

Besides my family, Jim Davis, my Junior Excellence coach, pushed me pretty hard. Davis may have been one of the first instructors to utilize videotape. His program helped me better understand the game and how to work hard, both physically and mentally. Jim was pretty strict. He wasn't easy on me. He sent a letter to my parents one time explaining why he was hard on me. He thought I had the makings of a great player so he wanted to bring out the best in me. I'm thankful for that. While tough, he did want us to improve. My lessons lasted sixty minutes a couple of times a week in addition to junior training.

Saturday mornings year-round we had challenge matches. No matter how hot in the summer or cold in the winter, we'd play matches against each other to improve our position on the ranking ladder. I don't remember if I ascended to the top of that ladder, but later I was ranked

No. 1 in northwest Ohio, No. 1 on my high school team, and No. 1 at the University of Toledo in both singles and doubles.

My brother also encouraged me to work hard and not give up. That meant a lot coming from my older brother. I owe a lot to him. He was—and still is—a gifted athlete, excelling in tennis, baseball, and golf. In high school, he had to pick one sport and he selected baseball. He was our star third baseman and All-Great Lakes League in 1979 and 1980. He also finished second in hitting both years. Dad and I rarely missed a game, often eating peanuts on the bleachers during Jim's home games. My brother's accomplishments academically and athletically inspired me.

When our family vacationed at the cottage on Canadian Lakes in Big Rapids, Michigan, Jim fed me a lot of tennis balls for hours on end. That may sound like we had fun hitting the ball back and forth to each other. I thought it was boring, but I did it anyway. We didn't just hit balls to each other; we had a purpose to what we did.

A tennis player has to work on a number of different strokes and that's what we did, day in and day out, hour after hour. Sometimes we'd hit for three hours, working on different skills. Footwork, conditioning, running are a few of the things a tennis player must learn in order to be great. You've got different grips and adjustments, different shot selections, strategy, and tactics.

I think one of the most important aspects of making a champion tennis player is the mental side of the sport. To be mentally tough, I relied on hero stories from inspirational books and movies like *Rocky* and *Rudy*. I love the stories of ordinary individuals who overcome tremendous adversity to accomplish their extraordinary dreams.

Another movie, *The Sword and the Sorcerer*, helped propel me to victory in the 1984 high school state doubles qualifier. Jim and I watched the movie about a medieval prince the night before the big match. Whoever won would move on to the state championships at Ohio State University in Columbus.

Before I stepped on the court and later when serving for match point, I remembered Jim that morning pumping his fist with an encouraging look while he said, "Talon, Talon, Talon." My partner and I reached match point. Tied 4-4 in a nine-point tie-breaker, I stepped to the line to serve. Naturally a person has certain thoughts and feelings right before a crucial time in any sporting event. What a person draws on from their memory bank makes the difference in winning or losing. That day I remembered the hero, Prince Talon, from the movie. I stepped to the line to serve. A scene from the movie flashed through my mind: Prince Talon plied himself free from the crucifix with much pain and agony and defeated the enemy. This scene chased away the jitters and negative thoughts. I've learned it's important to think in such a way that will help you win. If a person thinks about something negative, like missing a shot, then he most likely will. I get myself fired up drawing from my memories—good memories, or a positive vision of the future. While I stood on the baseline, I visualized serving to my opponent's backhand and going to the net to volley. The whole series played out exactly as I had seen it in my mind. We won the point, the match, and a spot in the state championships.

My partner and I raised our hands in victory. We jumped up and down because we were on our way to the state championships. At states, we made it to the semi-finals before bowing out to a strong Upper Arlington duo in a hard-fought match.

Becoming a champion is about what you have stored in your memory banks. Do you have garbage stored or do you think winning thoughts? The New Life Version of Proverbs 23:7 says, "For as he thinks in his heart, so is he." I didn't know that verse back then, but it means a lot to me now as a believer.

Mental toughness—in any sport—is huge. That's why when I first started playing tennis I never won. I got beaten by girls. I got beaten by my mom. I got beaten by everybody. And it made me mad. I'd throw my racquet, kick the net, or punch my strings. My temper was something I had to overcome. I believe a person learns a lot about who they are when they play a sport.

On some weekends, we'd pack the family station wagon, and head off for tournaments throughout the Midwest. We packed the car like we'd be there all day Saturday and Sunday. For the longest time, I got beaten in the first round. When that happened, because there's no reason to stay, we'd head back home. I realized my family believed in me to go to all this trouble and expense.

The turning point came at a weekend tournament when my first-round opponent didn't show up. Making it to the second round gave me a shot of confidence. It didn't matter that I advanced because of a forfeit. I was in the second round and my name was printed on the next bracket with the other winners of the first round. I don't recall if I won that tournament or not. I don't think I did. We stayed a little longer that weekend and enjoyed the extra tennis and eating out as a family. Eight years after I took my first tennis lesson, I finally managed to win a local tournament in Sylvania. I still have that trophy.

It took time for me to appreciate the game. I have much more patience now than when I was growing up. Improving at tennis is a process, like building a physical body. You don't see results the first day or two, but if you keep pounding away and focusing on what you hope to accomplish day after day, week after week, year after year, you'll eventually achieve the results you want.

I made my high school varsity team as the only freshman. My first match was a doubles match. I still remember my anxiety as we got ready. My heart raced and my palms sweated. My partner, a senior, had more experience and helped me settle down and play the game. I also remember the encouragement I received from my teammates. I'm thankful to our coach, Mr. Perry the school's history teacher, for giving me a spot on the varsity team even though I played only a few times during the season. I worked hard the next two years and was rewarded by playing line one my senior year in 1983.

I received the No. 1 singles ranking in Northwest Ohio and the No. 3 doubles ranking in the Western Tennis Association. I'll never forget the boys' 18-and-under clay court finals at the Toledo Tennis Club versus Doug Linden on July 21, 1983. Doug was very consistent and returned a lot of balls. This meant running and sliding on the clay for extended periods of time. If you don't drink a lot of water you can cramp up. We battled back and forth during the heat of the day until I served at match point. When I stood behind the baseline to prepare to serve for the match, my legs locked up. That is the worst pain imaginable. I took a timeout. Inside the men's locker room I was given salt tablets, fluids, and bananas to relieve the cramping. When the pain subsided, with the help of family and friends I got up and made it to the baseline to serve. If I went for too much, I might cause my legs to lock up again. I could still feel tingles running throughout my thighs, calves, and hamstrings. I decided to tap a serve into the service box and hope Doug would miss. Instead I hit the ball right to Doug and he blocked the ball back to me. I hobbled over to return it, hopefully for the last time. Doug netted the ball, giving me the championship. The newspaper headline the next day read: Minns stretches for net crown. After the match, I had to lay flat on my back for quite a while until the fluids, salt, and potassium kicked in and the cramps subsided. Despite my success in high school and junior tennis, no college scholarship offers came my way.

I ended up staying at home and attending the University of Toledo. I tried out for the tennis team my freshman year and was awarded a walk-on scholarship. Each college team has six singles lines and three doubles lines. We played challenge matches to determine who made it on the team and their positions in the lineup. I won enough challenge matches to earn the No. 3 singles spot and No. 2 doubles spot. I finished the season with a winning record, and enjoyed being a part of the college tennis experience.

College was difficult academically for me with all the class work, meeting with tutors and note takers, tennis

practice, going to the gym, and studying in the library. Reading lips all day exhausted both my eyes and mind. Many nights I took a quick nap in the study booths at the library.

I enjoyed the recognition I received in the university newspaper, as well as the local *Toledo Blade*. Because of it, my confidence increased as a tennis player and person. Oftentimes while I worked out at the gym, guys teased me because my name was in the paper a lot after a match or winning a tournament. Chuckling, they asked if my dad worked for the newspaper.

My hearing challenge took a back seat to the success I was achieving on the court. I still struggled in my classes though. Many of the classes in college were much larger and the professor used a microphone. This didn't help me because I rely on reading lips. My college counselor, Al Grande, found graduate assistants to work with me, listened to my fears and concerns, and consoled and encouraged me.

I remember this large class, on government, I think. The professor required the students to write their names on a note card. During each lecture he'd draw a name from the stack of cards and ask a question about the current discussion. When I understood the need for the cards, I hoped my name wouldn't be called because I couldn't hear or understand the discussions. Whenever he called a name, I'd look around to see who raised their hand. One day he called my name. When no one else responded, I asked, "Did you say Brad Minns?"

"Yes that's right," he said.

"That's me." A number of emotions—dread, embarrassment, humiliation, doubt, fear, worry, and hopelessness—surged through my mind. To battle those thoughts, I reminded myself of something my dad often told me while growing up. He said I have something most people don't: charisma. Over and over throughout the years, those words reverberated through my mind until I came to believe them. I used my charisma to overcome difficult and embarrassing situations.

The instructor asked me a question. He may as well have been speaking a foreign language since I couldn't understand what he said. I smiled and told him I had no idea what the class was discussing. I cracked a joke to lighten the mood. Then he remembered my hearing challenge and asked someone else the question.

Beginning my sophomore year, as well as my junior and senior years, I played line one in singles and doubles on the Toledo Rockets team. Playing line one singles and doubles in the Mid-American Conference was tough. Many great tennis players dotted the rosters in the league. Some were nationally ranked. Yet, I still managed winning seasons at my lines and improved as a tennis player.

All those years of repeatedly going through difficult situations on and off the tennis court helped me to overcome obstacles and grow more confident in myself and group dealings.

"I have always considered tennis as a combat in an arena between two gladiators who have their racquets and their courage as their weapons."
Yannick Noah

Chapter 4 | Playing Tennis After College

My playing career didn't end in college. Besides winning the Gold medal in the 1985 World Games for the Deaf in Los Angeles, I won numerous medals —Gold, Silver and Bronze—in other U.S. and International deaf events for singles, doubles, and mixed doubles.

In 1989 the World Games for the Deaf were held in Christchurch, New Zealand, one of the most beautiful places I've been. I loved the rolling hills covered with sheep grazing in the green pastures. I felt like I was living in an Irish Spring soap commercial. Kiwi fruit was served daily at lunch time. I wish someone would have told me sooner not to eat the skin on the outside the kiwi fruit.

A field was next to the school where we were housed. Athletes played cricket, sunbathers worked on their tans, and others relaxed and read books. Every morning I ran laps around the field to keep my conditioning strong. I was unable to locate a gym in the area, so I found an old inner tube from a bicycle tire, then used a pair of scissors to cut one end of the tube. This allowed me to do exercises like bicep curls, lateral raises, and triceps extensions. One night, a few of my teammates and I were playing catch with a tennis ball. An intended receiver missed one of my throws and the ball crashed through a dorm window. The following day as our team walked onto the practice courts, a cat walked along the edge of a fence about forty yards away. Acting a little cocky, I jokingly motioned to my teammates that I could hit the cat with a tennis ball. Not expecting to hit the cat from that distance. I tossed the ball, set my racquet back then proceeded to fire the ball across about three courts. The ball struck the cat in the ribs. My jaw practically hit the ground, I could hardly believe it. My teammates all looked at me with that "what do you think you're doing look." I felt bad and immediately apologized to my teammates. The cat was fine, just a little startled.

This time I was the defending champion and probably a little over-confident going into the tournament. Well, maybe not too overconfident. A few months before our training began in California, I was playing racquetball and sprained my ankle. It was the worst pain I've ever experienced. Throughout the New Zealand Olympics a trainer taped my ankle then covered it with an air-cast. But this wasn't going to stop me or slow me down.

A new challenger, Ronald Krieg from Germany, had arrived on the scene. I learned later that Krieg means "war" in German. That is exactly what it seemed like when we played against each other for the first time in the semifinal match. I'd heard Krieg played against former No. 1 champion Boris Becker back in their native country. Krieg, a red-headed, stocky, strong player with a short backswing and flicking type groundstroke, was difficult to play against.

For the second straight Deaf Olympic Games, I found myself serving at match point in a five-set battle. Instead of thinking about the Prince Talon scene or *Rocky*, I had a guilty conscience. I had a girlfriend back in Toledo, but couldn't stop thinking about an attractive New Zealand girl I'd met and had been spending time with during my stay. When I stepped to the line, I thought, "Should I serve easy, get the first serve in, keep the pressure on and hope he succumbs to the pressure, or go for the big ace?" I went the safe route and paid for it dearly. Krieg whipped the return right back and ended up winning in five sets.

I learned that I enjoy the thrill of victory a lot more than the agony of defeat. When I played for the bronze, I struggled to get pumped up to play because in my book the only thing that mattered was first place. I did manage to pull through, defeating a steady Swedish player to win the bronze medal. At the closing ceremonies, I noticed a number of the Swedish athletes had bumps on their upper lips. I thought they might have gotten fat lips because of a fight. When I was a little closer I could see that it was tobacco. During our time in New Zealand, I looked everywhere for some smokeless tobacco to satisfy a nasty habit. Nowhere in all Christchurch was I able to find any. I walked up to the Swedish team and explained to them that they had it all wrong. I said, "Give me your can." Once the can was in my hands I snapped the top with my first finger so it made a snapping sound to pack the tobacco tight. They watched attentively. I proceeded to pinch some tobacco into my lower lip "See this is how we do it in the USA," I said. Some tried to put their new found knowledge into action. It turned out to be a smokeless tobacco summit. Afterwards we all laughed, danced, and celebrated for the remainder of the closing ceremony.

I skipped the Sofia, Bulgaria, Games in 1993, but decided to play in the 1997 Games in Copenhagen, Denmark. I trained hard to stay in shape, hit some balls, and played in a few tournaments before flying to Copenhagen.

Our coach was Richard Pèpe, a great friend and restaurateur from Carmel, California. Travelling overseas with Pèpe is always fun. Pèpe got involved in the World Games for the Deaf one year as Kerry Belser's coach. Belser has played for USA since I started competing in the World Games for the Deaf and Dresse Cups in 1985. Pèpe was well-liked among our team and players from other countries as well, especially the Italians. During the trip to Copenhagen, he introduced me to coffee. Since riding a bike or walking was our main mode of transportation, we walked home from the tennis courts at night. Pèpe would stop at coffee shops or bakeries scouting out the various delicacies and coffees. One night he offered me an espresso. I couldn't resist. The aroma and cool looks of the tiny cups seemed like the thing to do in Copenhagen. The hot espresso gave me a caffeine buzz that helped me to stay awake during the long walks home. I've enjoyed drinking black coffee and espresso ever since.

The matches in Denmark were challenging. After battling through a few rounds in singles, doubles and mixed doubles, I again found myself on the opposite side of the net from Krieg. I fell behind two sets to none and won the next two sets, forcing the decisive fifth set. This time, he beat me easily. After Krieg shook my hand he turned around and drew a heart in the red clay with his tennis racquet. I wondered what was going on as he spelled out the words, "Will you marry me?" His fiancée burst into tears while running onto the court to say "yes." Watching Krieg's proposal and the joy on their faces seemed  to take some of the sting out of my loss that day.

Although Krieg had beaten me twice now in singles competition, my partner Jay Smithley, a great college player from Indiana, and I were able to win the gold at Copenhagen in men's doubles against Krieg and his partner. Krieg and I were given less than an hour following the five-set singles match before we had to play the gold medal doubles match on the same court. I felt sore, tired, hungry, and defeated when the match started. I told Jay he'd have to hold me up and play a little harder for us to win. He did, making some great poaching volleys, serving and volleying to perfection while I did my best to help him. We found ourselves down and—much to the delight of the mostly German crowd—on the verge of defeat. Many of our American fans thought we were done and left. Our only support came from Coach Pèpe who raised a small American flag every time we won a point.

Eventually, I found my second wind. I no longer felt sore, tired or hungry. I only thought about winning the match. We fought hard and came from behind to win the Gold medal.

Good things happen when you refuse to quit.

The next day at breakfast we saw some of the

spectators who had left the match early. Thinking we'd lost, they tried to sympathize and console us.

"What are you talking about," I said. "We came back and won."

It seemed that an unseen hand carried me through the match. It was damp, rainy, and dreary except for a brief moment when the clouds parted and the sun shone brightly when Jay and I were given our medals. I shed a tear, looked into the sky and thanked God for allowing me to be a part of an extraordinary event while representing an extraordinary country.

In addition to the World Games for the Deaf, which are held every four years, the Dresse Cup is held for deaf tennis players every two years. It brings deaf tennis players from different countries to compete in this prestigious event, with a single purpose which is to promote the culture of friendship and to test the strength of the top elite tennis players in a team format.

Started in 1960 by Antonine Dresse of Belgium, the Dresse Cup is patterned after the Davis Cup. The Dresse Cup is the deaf equivalent to the Davis Cup. In Davis Cup, each country brings their very best players to compete against each other. Not for money, fame or selfish ambition, but for the pure love and joy of tennis and country.

When the Dresse Cup tournament came to the Nick Bollettieri Tennis Academy in Bradenton, Florida, the U.S.

The Dresse Cup-winning American team (from left): Coach Rich Pepe, Jeff Ploederl, Jamie McElfresh, Brad Minns and Jay Smithley. It was the first time the Americans won in the 35-year history of the Dresse Cup.

team, led by Coach Pèpe, sought to end its thirty-five-year winless drought. Krieg and I battled in another tough singles match. He won, 7-6, 0-6, 6-4. Coach Pèpe decided to play Jay Smithley and me against the strong German doubles team of Krieg and his partner. Jay and I fought off the Germans' challenge, winning in three sets, 6-1, 3-6, 6-4, to give the U.S. its first Dresse Cup in history. Winning the Dresse Cup meant a lot when the USA flag appeared on the list of champions for the first time in Cup history.

My family had high hopes for me. They knew I had it in me to be a great tennis player. And they were right.

Over the years I've enjoyed some wonderful achievements, much more than I first expected. I've grown to love the game, have become more patient, and learned many valuable life lessons. That's why I coach now, to help others learn and to love the game as much as I do.

"One man has enthusiasm for thirty minutes, another for thirty days, but it is the man who has it for thirty years who makes a success of his life."
Edward B. Butler

Chapter 5 | Bodybuilding

Weightlifting transformed my life and my tennis game. Without it, I probably wouldn't have become the person I am today or won the tough matches I did. Before I began lifting weights I lacked self-confidence. I didn't believe I could win because of a weak mindset and felt having hearing aids put me at a disadvantage.

When I was thirteen, my brother Jim inspired me after he developed a strong, athletic physique to help with his baseball game in high school. He often threw a flex of his bicep which had incredible peak and he was also the proud owner of a set of washboard abs that he developed with the weights in our basement. I began to think that if weightlifting helped him to improve his game, then maybe it could help me to become a better tennis player and boost my self-esteem.

My passion for weightlifting began one day while shopping with my mother at the local mall. That day I saw Arnold Schwarzenegger's book, *The Education of a*

Bodybuilder, near the front of the bookstore. I'd never seen a bodybuilder before. Naturally I was curious and picked up the book. Arnold exuded self-confidence and power—things I desired—in the cover shot. This guy had muscles. Me? I was a skinny guy with two big bulky hearing aids. The book wasn't very long and included photos of the exercises and a basic nutrition plan. When Mom found me, I asked if she would buy the book for me.

She asked one question. "Are you going to read it?"

Of course, I answered I would. And I did. I probably finished that book faster than any other I'd read up to that point in my life. I love books. Because of my hearing impairment, I read a lot back then and still do today. I loved spending time at a library or a bookstore. When I finished reading it I went down into our basement where my brother kept an old set of Joe Weider weights, the ones with a plastic covering around concrete. Those weights were popular back then. It seemed everyone owned a set. I started applying some of my new-found knowledge about weightlifting and began visualizing the way I wanted to look. From the books I'd read I discovered great athletes believe in themselves and their abilities. I also learned they visualize their success, believe they will succeed and then do. I visualized myself having muscles, being stronger and more confident. I thought if Schwarzenegger can come to the United States, speaking very little English, with hardly any contacts or money, then build his body and make a name for himself, then why can't I? So, I started building a better body.

I discovered I loved working out. The first time I picked up the weights became a life-changing moment for me. I was hooked. Lifting became my passion. I daydreamed about building up my body, being stronger and bigger. So I focused most of my time and energy lifting weights, reading bodybuilding magazines, and eating non-stop in an effort to put on some weight.

Brother Jim stressed the importance of writing down goals and reaffirming them out loud throughout the day until it became ingrained in my memory. I constantly repeated to myself that I'd be the state tennis champion. The more I lifted weights, the stronger my body became. I also realized an additional benefit to weightlifting: a stronger mindset. I believed I could beat the guy on the other side of the net because I felt I was stronger and better prepared, even if his strokes were better. I believed I possessed a huge mental edge.

A neighborhood friend, Dirk Boyles, soon became my workout partner. He also had a gym in his basement. Nearly every day after school we'd be in his basement or mine working out. Having a training partner motivates you to push a little harder, more so than when training alone. The discipline I developed in the basement gym carried over onto the tennis courts and I started to win against players who had previously beaten me. I learned winning is a habit that takes daily dedication, commitment to excellence, discipline, and a never-give-up determination.

A group of neighborhood friends noticed a change in Dirk and me and joined our workouts. We pushed each other. We chided each other. We bulked up. We tried drinking raw eggs like Rocky Balboa. However, I failed that test and haven't tried since. But we took our training seriously. Back in those days, when most kids went to a party or school dance, I preferred a small group of gym buddies, laughing, hanging out, and having a good time. Background noise and the difficulty of reading lips in large crowds, such as parties and dances, diminished my desire to attend those events. Reading lips can be exhausting. Some people's lips are harder to read than others. I prefer a person speak in a normal tone of voice without slowing down or deliberately trying to communicate.

We worked out for several years in our basements before we moved our training routine to the newest exercise equipment, Nautilus. Arthur Jones, who created Nautilus, helped change the public's perception about bodybuilding and strength-training exercise. Jones' High Intensity Training method involved short, single sets with maximum intensity, a much different approach than Schwarzenegger's training method that involved  hours in the gym using free weights. We did Nautilus machines for a while, until we saw Arnold's movie,

Pumping Iron, in 1977. After that we headed to Gold's Gym in Sylvania.

The moment I stepped into the local Gold's, I was amazed. I loved that place and still do. I loved the sights, smells and sounds of the hardcore body building activity. People slammed their weights, shouted encouragement to their workout partners, and the smell of Ben Gay filled the air. Men and women wrapped their knees and put on their belts to do heavy sets, much like a warrior preparing for battle. Gold's was the first place I ever went that I immediately felt like I was at home away from home. Of all the gyms I've worked out at in the United States and abroad, the Sylvania Gold's remains my favorite because of the great memories and the people. It later became OJ's gym and then the Weight Station and is now a distant memory.

My buddies and I arrived each day after dinner around 7:00 p.m. The same group of people showed up consistently around the same time to work out, laugh, and have a good time. I met some of my best friends at that gym. Our workouts lasted anywhere from sixty to ninety minutes. Afterwards, we'd load up on carbo force drinks, which came in these

cool plastic bottles and tasted like Kool-Aid, and ate delicious home-made protein filled breads.

At Gold's, I discovered another level of weightlifting. One of my first impressions was the forty-five-pound Olympic bar. In the basement, we used those skinny plastic bars. I thought I could lift anything, so I grabbed an Olympic bar hoping to pound out a bunch of reps. Trying to balance that bar made me feel uncoordinated and weak. In the beginning, I could barely bench sixty-five pounds, but I eventually got to 285, but short of my goal of 315.

I enjoyed being at the gym, which was important to me. Here I was a young teenager, with two big hearing aids hanging on the back of my ears, feeling like I found a place to fit in. It was a place where everyone supported and encouraged each other to reach their individual goals.

In the gym, I applied the lessons of goal setting, visualization and perseverance and continued to grow physically and mentally stronger. Day after day, week after week, month after month, year after year, working out never got boring to me. I was building a better physique and adding more muscle. At the same time, I was gaining a lot of self-confidence which gave me hope for the future. As a result, I started to dream of all the things I wanted to accomplish in my life.

For a while, the stuff I learned from Arnold's book became a way of life for me. I was inspired by Schwarzenegger. To me, he had everything a person could want. He was enthusiastic about life, always appeared to be laughing, and had a lot of self-confidence. He overcame a lot of adversity to come here from Austria. Because he worked hard he eventually became a successful business man, a champion bodybuilder, the star in the "Terminator" franchise, married a famous woman (Maria Shriver), and served as the governor of California for eight years.

He demonstrated what it takes to achieve success. At that time, those were the things I strived for. That's what I wanted ... to be successful, well-liked. I wanted to have nice things, confidence, all the stuff Schwarzenegger seemed to be getting.

My dedication to lifting weights paid off in several areas of my life. Winning became a way of life. My self-confidence skyrocketed. I was no longer afraid to ask girls out on dates. Before graduating from high school, I dated the prettiest girl in high school, the same girl who I was afraid to speak to years earlier.

Because of his impact on my life, one of my goals was to meet Arnold in person. I had written this goal down along with many other goals. Looking back, I probably went a little overboard in that effort. When my girlfriend at the time moved out west, I moved to California, near Venice Beach where Arnold worked out with some of the other top bodybuilders, guys like Franco Columbo, Lou Ferrigno, Frank Zane, and Dennis Tinerino. Venice Beach was, and still is, the mecca of bodybuilding. I wanted to go there to experience the same things he had experienced. And maybe, just maybe, I would get the chance to meet him.

I found some deaf friends in Northridge and lived with them. Hoping to meet Arnold, the hour drive to Venice Beach each day went quickly. Muscle beach was just as I'd imagined it. A small area still remained in the sand littered with old rusty weights, possibly the same ones the bodybuilding greats used during the '70s heyday of bodybuilding. Along the beach path, a number of entertainers, probably dreaming of being the next guest on *The Tonight Show*, gave the crowds a show. I also got a few workouts in at the Venice Beach Gold's Gym, where it all began. The size of Gold's Venice overwhelmed me. Row after row of every machine made was available. Tons of free weights were racked up neatly along the perimeter of the gym. The walls contained photographs of many of the bodybuilding greats. It was an incredible sensation to be there and train where the best bodybuilders still come from all over the world. One day while I set up to do some dead lifts, a couple of bulked up women asked if they could join me. "Sure, no problem," I said. After warming up with 135 then going up to maybe 285 or 315, I realized these ladies were still going up in weight and reps. After a few sets, and feeling out of my league, I dismissed myself and moved on to some other exercises. About every person there looked as if they could have been on the cover of a muscle magazine. After training at Gold's and enjoying some time at the beach, I headed up to the campus of UCLA. I remembered from the '85 World Games for the Deaf how big the buffet was at the cafeteria. I was looking to bulk up after seeing a number of oversized bodybuilders at Gold's

and this seemed like the place to eat.

I didn't achieve my goal of meeting Arnold while in California. Years later, my goal to meet Arnold finally materialized. Ironically, the dream came true in my home state of Ohio, after winning the Physique Augmentation System (PAS) Bodybuilding Championships, now known as the popular Body for Life developed by Bill Phillips. We met backstage, shook hands, and said a few words. Meeting my boyhood inspiration was a thrill of a lifetime.

As I've said before, my main goal in weightlifting was to build my body and get bigger and stronger. When I felt physically stronger, I felt mentally stronger. I felt better about myself. I became physically stronger so I could win at tennis. I wanted to develop confidence and I did. I didn't care how good my opponent was or his ranking; I believed I could outlast him as a result of all my physical training. I developed a champion's mindset. No matter what my opponent threw at me, I kept fighting back until I wore him out.

Tennis professionals and coaches discouraged me from lifting weights. My coaches thought it'd hurt my game. Lifting helped my game, both physically and mentally. Nowadays most professional tennis players incorporate weightlifting into their training regimen. Andy Murray, for instance, made it to the top in the rankings by committing to a disciplined program and hiring former champion Ivan Lendl to be his coach. Lendl was one of the first tennis players to help pave the way for the modern era of "power tennis."

Weightlifting opened many doors and helped me gain the confidence I needed to overcome the adversity of being hearing challenged in a hearing world. The lessons I learned—commitment, goal-setting, visualizing, hard work and perseverance, when applied by following a consistent weightlifting program—helped me accomplish many of my goals and dreams.

Today, I am just as passionate about weightlifting as I was when I first started more than thirty-five years ago. I train with machines, free weights, medicine balls, Swiss balls and bands in our home gym, and am committed to living a fitness lifestyle. As a certified personal trainer, I teach and encourage others to get fit and go for their dreams.

Having a mental edge is something that takes time to develop. No one is born with it. Mental toughness comes from being around positive people and reading the books that inspire and motivate. Both of these impact the way you think. It's about believing in yourself. If you don't, there's no purpose or point in stepping onto the court. If you don't think you can defeat your opponent, there's no point in playing. Winning a tennis match takes place before you step onto the court. You probably could say that about a lot, if not all, other sports as well.

You have to believe you can beat the guy on the other side of the net. It doesn't matter if he is ranked No. 1 in the country. If you don't think you'll beat him, you won't. At some point in my life I developed a belief system that I could beat anybody. When that happened, I felt I could do anything. This mindset was constantly being reinforced by my coaches and family. I encourage you to read good books and watch motivational movies. The *Rocky* movies helped me, and I'm sure you might already know a movie or two that can help you and give you the mental edge needed to be victorious.

If you hang around people who talk defeat, it becomes difficult to win. People who don't believe in themselves won't believe in you. Your friends can make you or break you. So choose your friends wisely.

Not until I started bodybuilding did I have confidence that carried over onto the tennis courts. All that strength and confidence I got from lifting helped me to be the tennis player and person that I am today.

"The mediocre teacher tells. The good teacher explains.
The superior teacher demonstrates.
The great teacher inspires."
William Arthur Ward

Chapter 6 | Becoming a Tennis Pro

One of the greatest feelings I ever experienced was walking down the platform to receive my college degree from the University of Toledo with a Bachelor of Science degree in Sports Administration and Consumer Relations. I breathed a huge sigh of relief as my family and friends congratulated me on a remarkable job. It was now time to find my career.

The summer after graduating from college, I took tennis teaching jobs at St. James Club and the Courts of Sylvania Tennis Club where I honed my tennis teaching skills. I learned a lot by observing the other pros, but I still needed much improvement. I decided to sign up for Dennis Van der Meer's weeklong Tennis University in Hilton Head Island, S.C. Van der Meer is known as "the coach's coach" and has taught countless teaching pros the standard method of teaching tennis, which breaks down each stroke into basic, easy-to-remember steps that make tennis easier to learn and much more fun.

I booked a flight to Savannah, Georgia, and was picked up by a mini-bus which drove me the remaining forty-five miles or so to the island in January 1989. As a teenager, I had vacationed at Hilton Head with my Aunt Nancy, Uncle John, and my cousins Paula and Mark, along with a grade school teacher and her family. I loved Hilton Head the first time I visited there with my cousins and was excited to be back, yet nervous about the upcoming teaching seminar. Similar thoughts of worry, doubt, and "what if" began to creep into my mind. Again I needed to persevere if I was to become a certified tennis teaching professional.

The next morning while having breakfast at the Days Inn where I stayed, I found myself among many other tennis pros from around the world who also had signed up for the course. Tennis pros are fairly easy to distinguish simply by looking at their shoes, tennis shorts, warm-up jackets and bulky bags hanging from their shoulders. I wondered how I measured up to the other pros in terms of communicating on the court, teaching groups, and hearing what the students and other coaches said—all the same things I have dealt with growing up while attending hearing schools.

After breakfast, we headed over to the Van der Meer World Tennis Center. Some pros sat and others stood along the fences of the first court while we waited for our instructor. Van der Meer arrived with his trademark whistle around his neck and smile on his face. He greeted each of us and asked for our names. I don't know how he did it, but by the end of the day he knew every single person's name. I've struggled with this. Sometimes I have to ask a person's name several times before I get it. Even then I might not get it right. I've improved at this over the years, but still strive to do better.

The Tennis University course consisted of classroom discussions which covered all areas of tennis from rules, court dimensions, tennis ratings, strategy, tactics, etc. I asked the gentleman behind me, Carlos, if I could see his notes to keep up with the class. We later ended up in the same group for the on-court teaching portion. Today, Carlos is one of my closest friends. He still teases me about a funny incident that happened at the University. One day our group was told to take turns giving each other a lesson on different strokes. One of the keys of being a good instructor is the ability to find flaws in a person's game and then instruct that player on how to improve. The group lined up at the baseline and we each hit a forehand. Next the student/teacher critiqued our form and gave us the appropriate correction. When the student instructor got around to me, he asked, "Brad, uh let's see, what's your problem?" I looked at Carlos, he looked at me and we did our best to hold back our laughter. I finally blurted, "No problem here, bro." That set Carlos off as he struggled to contain his laughter. Now more than twenty-five years later, every time I get a letter or email from Carlos, somewhere he asks, "Brad what's your problem?"

After we learned the standard method of teaching, the next phase was to teach tennis to the locals who lived on the island. Van der Meer advertised free tennis lessons to anyone who wanted them. This gave our class the opportunity to test our skills and gain confidence teaching tennis.

At the end of the week, and after many hours in the class room and on the courts, it was time to be tested. The

PTR test consisted of a written exam, racquet grips test, tennis skills test, teaching a group, and teaching a private lesson. We were to be certified at different levels, depending on how well we scored. I crammed though the manual, refreshing my memory of the details we'd gone over for the week and felt confident, although I was a little worried about remembering the names of the students in my class.

Van der Meer, his wife Pat, and the entire staff made each one of us feel like we were the best, which helped when it came to the final exam. I finished my testing, then went back to the hotel, walked the beach, ate a nice dinner, and returned to the hotel. I couldn't sleep that night because I was excited to see if I'd reached my dream of becoming a certified tennis teaching professional. I learned a lot and felt much more confident as a tennis instructor. In the back of my mind I wanted to move to Hilton Head someday. Despite my dream to move to the island, I was excited to get home to Toledo and apply everything I had learned. The next day they passed out the test results and I learned I'd indeed become a USPTR certified tennis pro with the level of instructor.

I flew back home and shared the good news with my family, then went back to work at the clubs. I taught for a few months, but the desire to move to Hilton Head continued to tug at my heart. Finally, one day I told my family I was going to go back to Hilton Head and look for a tennis teaching job on the island.

I packed my bags and drove my black Toyota pickup truck from Toledo to South Carolina. The drive took all day. By the time I arrived darkness blanketed the area and made it difficult to drive on the back roads leading to the island. I hadn't made any sleeping arrangements and thought I might have to sleep in my truck. Instead, I went to the same hotel where I stayed during the Tennis University class. After explaining to the night deskman what I was there to do, he offered me an extended stay discount rate.

The next morning, I created my résumé and distributed it to about every possible place where there was a tennis court on the island. My desire, however, was to teach at Sea Pines Plantation, former home of the Family Circle Cup, a popular women's pro tennis event. After talking with Bunny Williams, the manager at Sea Pines, she informed me a new pro had been hired days before.

I was offered a teaching position elsewhere, but because of my dream to work at Sea Pines I held off on taking it. I loved Sea Pines, and still do.

Years earlier I experienced one of the highlights of my life. While vacationing there with my relatives, my  Uncle John had arranged for me to play tennis with tennis legend Stan Smith, a former number one ranked tennis player in the world. Today, Stan, along with Billy Stearns, leads the Smith-Stearns Tennis Academy at Sea Pines. I decided to give it one last try to see if I could get a job at Sea Pines. I went back and spoke to Bunny. With much enthusiasm I explained to her how much the place felt like home to me. I enthusiastically convinced her I'd be a good addition to their staff. It must have been a good pitch because she hired me. I was excited about this new position. I phoned home on my TTY telephone, which is a telephone for the deaf. To use a TTY I call a relay operator and the operator calls the number I requested. The receiving party answers the phone and speaks to the relay operator, and the operator types back what they said. This phone was a blessing to me, but it's difficult to arrange lessons and set up clinics because a lot of people didn't understand it. You see, the operator usually greets the caller with "Hello this is the relay service. Are you familiar with the service?" Before I had a chance to tell a potential client what I am calling about, sometimes to my dismay, they'd hang up.

I was happy to be a pro at Sea Pines where I taught the Stroke of the Day, conducted the Stan Smith Jr. Tennis Academy, and taught private and group lessons. We taught a lot of students during the summer months. People from around the world came to stay on the island and play tennis so I had an opportunity to meet a lot of interesting people and improve my teaching skills. During the winter months not much happened on the island and it got pretty cold at times. As a young pro in my early twenties, single, and filled with dreams, I was too restless so I decided to return home to Toledo after a season on the island.

"Modeling is a profession where your worth
is tied up with looks."
Christy Turlington

Chapter 7 | Modeling

"Brad you should try to be a model." Those words
didn't register at first, but after failing to pass the pre-Series

7 exam to determine
whether or not I had the
necessary ability to become
a stockbroker, I thought,
how hard can it be? Having
previously passed the Ohio
State real estate exam by
one point called for
celebration, but realizing
how much work was done
over the phone, modeling
became more appealing to
me. The dream of modeling
began in the early 1990s
with the encouragement of

a friend. Everyone in my family thought it might be a good
idea also. They saw my passion for bodybuilding and
thought it would be a good fit for a modeling career. The
idea of being in the magazines appealed to me. My training
began after college when I enrolled in the six-month course
at the John Robert Powers School of Modeling in Detroit in

1989. I drove an hour—sometimes through snow or sleet—once a week to learn how to walk the runway and pose for pictures, as well as etiquette for fine dining, and proper dress and wardrobe. These lessons prepared me to be a gentleman.

Early on, our class instructor shared several stories of other male models that became successful. This generated a lot of hope and confidence that one day I could become a successful model. As far as I knew, no other deaf models had yet broken into the industry. This motivated me to train harder in the gym to get in the best shape possible.

The desire to become a model became so intense that I endured much more pain and pushed myself harder than ever before. After hundreds of roman chairs, sit-ups, hanging leg raises, bar twists, among many other abdominal exercises, I had chiseled out my abs. When I felt

I was in peak condition, I met with local photographers to take shots for my comp card. A comp card is a model's advertisement card that consists of measurements and several photographs, including a head shot, a fitness shot, and a lifestyle shot. The process of getting modeling jobs takes a considerable amount of time, money, and travel with no guarantees. However, in my mind, I had no doubt I could succeed. After all, I was different and I learned how to use those differences to my advantage. With the help of a local modeling agency, I was chosen out of many other models to do runway, catalogue, print work, and a few television commercials.

On the set, communication was difficult with other models, makeup artists, photographers, agents, and stage managers, especially when the photographer asked me to remove my hearing aids. Sometimes I tightened my face and frowned in an effort to see through the bright lights and read my photographer's lips to understand what he said. With time and experience, these obstacles soon became meaningless as my posing skills improved. Soon I became a comfortable and natural poser while I imagined myself posing like the beautiful Michael Angelo statues that I saw at the Toledo Art Museum. I took pride in my work and wanted to do my best to make the photographs perfect.

In an audition there can be hundreds of other models with great physiques for the same casting call. The actual photo shoot itself is the fun part. The final product, a handsome face or perfect body in an ad or on the cover of a magazine, is the result of a lot of time and effort that go into staying in shape, and following a strict nutritional plan. This means lots of salads, lean meats, fruits and vegetables, and plenty of water. Keeping my portfolio current meant updating my photographs, meeting with agents, and attending auditions. It can be disheartening to put in a lot of work and not get the job. The competition is tough, but I learned to persevere and never give up on my dream.

After modeling in the Midwest for a while, I headed to Miami, Florida, the hot bed for the top modeling agents, photographers, and models from around the world. I'd never seen so many beautiful faces and bodies before I arrived in Miami. Everyone seemed to have a model's look and the competition looked intimidating. I temporarily stayed with a friend from high school in his penthouse suite which overlooked Star Island and Gloria Estefan's beautiful home. He was an established photographer in the area who helped me get started in improving my portfolio. I thought the artistic black and white body shots he took were amazing. I hardly believed the man in those photos was me. After seeing these new photographs, my confidence skyrocketed as I thought I can do this.

Another friend, a local tennis pro at the Shawnee Beach Resort on South Beach near the famed Fontainebleau Hotel, showed me around and helped me get established in the area. I landed a job teaching tennis at Flamingo Park, home of the Orange Bowl Junior Tennis Championships. He also found me a place to live at a North Beach hotel in the process of being renovated. We talked to the manager about a room in exchange for work.

He said, "You can stay here if you clean my pool."

"Sure," I said.

Because no one used the pool, I worked on my tan by laying out every day. A few weeks into this new venture, I sensed someone leaning over me. I didn't hear anyone walk up because I'd taken out my hearing aids. I opened my eyes to see the manager.

"What are you doing?" he said.

"I'm working on my tan."

"I think we need to find you another job."

I went from pool cleaner to security guard, which included sharing desk duty with some other locals. These guys were big Spanish dudes with heavy accents and badges. I struggled to read lips in English and now I had to read lips in a foreign language. I was given a walkie-talkie for patrolling during the wee hours of the night. I guess my bosses didn't realize I couldn't hear them talking on it.

One night while on patrol in the hotel, I walked into the lower level. When I tried to exit through the front door I discovered it was locked. I then tried to leave through the back door, but it had locked behind me. Realizing the walkie-talkie was useless to me, all I could do was wait.

And I waited a long time before my backup came looking for me. I acted as if it was no big deal.

My life in Miami wasn't glamorous. My bathroom doubled as my kitchen. I cooked most of my meals with a small burner, and ate a lot of pasta and chicken. To supplement my meals, I drank protein shakes with the popular product known as "Hot Stuff" that all the local bodybuilders were drinking at the time. I did a lot of running to stay in shape in the event an agent or photographer called.

A lot of people helped me during my time in Miami. A local gym traded a free membership in exchange for a few photographs they used in their advertisements. This allowed me to train for free while building my portfolio. Irene Marie, a popular modeling agency in the area, assigned Stewart Shining, a budding photographer, to take some of my photos. We traded work to build our portfolios. He took the shots and I modeled. Shining is a very creative photographer who took amazing shots that helped me land work. Years later, Shining became known for his *Sports Illustrated* swimsuit photographs.

I didn't enjoy the Miami lifestyle. People liked to stay out late to party. I preferred going to bed early so I could get up and train. The party life wasn't for me, so with my portfolio complete, I went back home to Toledo.

My modeling career came to a sudden halt one rainy day after I finished a fashion show. While driving down the Ohio interstate I made a split-second decision to visit my realtor girlfriend at an open house she was hosting. As I tried to change lanes, the back of my Toyota pickup truck fishtailed and put me into a complete spin. I grabbed for my seatbelt while the truck headed for a guardrail. It hit hard and flipped over several times. My life flashed before my eyes. When the truck came to a halt, I was upside down in the passenger seat. Blood oozed into my eyes and all over my face and shirt. The first thing I did was to move my arms and legs. I was thankful I could move.

I wanted to get out of the truck, but a lady who had stopped to help said, "No you stay here and wait for an ambulance."

"Please don't tell my parents what happened," I said.

A few seconds later my mom stuck her head into the cab of the truck.

Wide eyed, I said to the lady, "I told you not to tell my parents."

Mom said, "No honey, I was driving on the other side of the expressway when I saw your truck in the middle of the road. I was on my way to Grandma's house."

I went to the hospital where they stitched my forehead up and bandaged my knuckles. Later a doctor realigned my eyebrows, which still are a little crooked. This was the first time I seriously thought about what would have happened if I had died. I felt I'd been given a second chance at life.

When my girlfriend's parents moved to another state, she and I moved to Florida around 1990. After staying in Jacksonville for a little bit, we decided Orlando might have more opportunities for my tennis and modeling careers. One of our cars broke down near Longwood. While it was in the repair shop, we looked for an apartment. Post Lake Apartments in nearby Apopka caught our attention. We fell in love with the beautifully landscaped complex with a lake view, lots of trees, two pools and four tennis courts. I went to see the manager to ask whether she would be willing to reduce our rent in exchange for tennis lessons.

She said, "That's amazing you asked, because the pro here is moving out this week." She gave us a great deal for a one-bedroom apartment on the third floor.

One day after we'd been there a while, thunder from an afternoon storm shook the apartment. At least I thought it was thunder. Our two cats looked at me funny as I continued to eat and watch television. Someone knocked on the door, and when I opened it, I saw fire trucks lined up in front of the building. Within an hour the apartment burned down and we were left with nothing but the cats and tennis racquets I managed to grab as I bolted out the door.

That winter, I attended the USPTR annual symposium and tennis tournament in Hilton Head, South Carolina. I was playing great tennis at the time and wasn't focusing much on bodybuilding or modeling. While there, my pager went off and between sets I checked to see who had contacted me. It was my modeling agent Doug Bailey from Orlando. He had left the longest page I ever received from him. As I scrolled through his long message, I could sense Doug's excitement so I figured something good was up. Finally, I read, "Brad, guess what? Bill Phillips picked your comp card from a whole stack of other comp cards." The message went on to say this was not an audition; this was an actual job. Phillips wanted me to model for PowerBlock, the home workout equipment that featured interlocking weights inside of each other.

Phillips was a popular figure in the bodybuilding world at the time. He started *Muscle Media 2000* magazine in March 1992 which stayed in print until 2004 when EAS (Experimental Applied Sciences) was sold a second time.

At its peak, more than 500,000 people subscribed to the magazine. Phillips, who is a gifted writer and passionate about bodybuilding, inspired millions of people to get healthy and is still doing that today. In 1997, he changed the name to *Muscle Media* and the focus shifted to more of a mainstream audience. Landing a job to work with Phillips was the most exciting opportunity yet.

After the symposium, I returned to Orlando, packed my bags, and flew to Denver, Colorado. The next morning a driver picked me up at the hotel and took me to Phillips' home in Golden, about thirty minutes west of Denver. Phillips also had selected a female model, Ami Cusack, to pose with me. Cusack later was a contestant on the television reality series *Survivor*. We shot for a full day at Phillips' house. The lower level of his house had a beautiful gym with framed photographs of Arnold throughout. I spent some time pumping up doing some push-ups, sit ups and squats before the photo shoot, but still didn't feel completely ready because I'd lost a lot of muscle weight during the tennis tournament at Hilton Head.

Cusack and I spent a lot of time waiting around for the photographer to get the lights in the right spot and everything set for the actual shoot. Finally, Phillips walked in, smiled, greeted us, and then left to go do some work.

Because Phillips didn't have much food and only water to drink in his refrigerator, we drank Met-Rx protein shakes with our shaker bottles throughout the day. Afterwards, I went back to the hotel, changed clothes, and later met Phillips and Cusack for dinner. We had a great time and I was on cloud nine just being there.

The next day I waited in the EAS office and talked with Brevin Adams, Phillips' right-hand man, while I waited for my ride to the airport. I noticed supplements I hadn't seen or heard of before: V2G, GKG, Phosphagen, and Phosphagain.

So I asked, "What is this stuff?"

Adams said they were the new supplements EAS was about to release into the market. He also mentioned EAS had a new competition called PAS that, if followed correctly in addition to the supplement schedule, one could add a lot of muscle in a short amount of time. "We'll be looking for our second spokesperson to represent EAS," he said.

Excited, I asked, "How do I sign up?"

I visualized myself as their next spokesperson and couldn't wait to enter the competition when I got back to Orlando. The winner would receive a $50,000 endorsement contract, a Corvette, a meeting with Arnold, and an opportunity to travel to the Arnold Classic in Columbus, Ohio and the Mr. Olympia Contest in Atlanta, Georgia.

I ordered the necessary supplements and followed that program to a "T". When I went out on weekends with friends, I remained disciplined with my regimen even if they were drinking alcohol and eating fried food. I'd sit there counting down the minutes until my next round of supplements and protein drinks. Usually every two to three hours.

Holidays can be a challenging time with all the parties and good food. But with a strong vision and passion to reach a goal, one can learn to say no to the things that stand in the way of reaching it. When I went home to Toledo for Thanksgiving dinner with the family, I made sure I had my Tupperware filled with my next meal—dry tuna, brown rice, and salsa. Of course, I declined the pecan and apple pies.

I applied the goal setting, visualization, and discipline that I learned from tennis and bodybuilding to help me push myself more than ever before. I told myself every day before I went to the gym that I was going to train harder than anyone else in the world.

Like many times before, I was determined to win the prize. Nothing would stop me. I worked hard in the gym lifting heavy weights, doing basic lifts like bench presses, squats, barbell rows, leg presses, and dead lifts. My weight increased from 169 to 191. My supplement routine was working great and the Outback steaks, baked potatoes (no butter) and salads never got old.

I went to Publix to weigh myself regularly. Even a hurricane that blew through Central Florida couldn't stop me from making my protein shakes. When the storm knocked out power in my apartment, I drove around town looking for someone with electricity. I discovered the nearby fire station had power. I walked in and asked if I could borrow some electricity to make my protein shake. A fireman lying on the sofa replied "Sure, go ahead."

At one point in my training, overanxious to add weight, I lifted too much and blew out my shoulder doing heavy bench presses. This discouraged me at first, and I wasn't sure what I was going to do. I finally regrouped and changed my strategy. I decided to give my shoulder time to heal but at the same time blasted away at lower body training with the goal of gaining more size and strength in my legs. To get my shoulder back to full strength, I spent a few weeks doing ice and heat therapy. I accomplished this by jumping in and out of the freezing pool and into the hot tub during the cold winter months.

My determination was at an all-time high. After about three weeks I was able to go full strength with the

barbell bench presses again. My mother was in town for a visit when I finished my ten weeks of training. When we went shopping at Publix, I weighed myself as usual. For the first time ever I reached my goal of 191 pounds.

When I reached my weight goal, I hired a professional photographer to meet me at World Gym to take my "after" photos. I showed up an hour before our appointment to pump up for the photo shoot. We took a lot of pictures in the gym. She finally said, "Well, we have five shots left, what would you like to do?"

I suggested we take the rest of the shots outside. A few days later I picked up the photos. I didn't like any of the indoor shots. Disappointed, I came to the outdoor shots. I loved them! They were exactly what I needed. I chose one and sent off my before and after shots. I felt confident that I would be trading in my Honda for a Corvette in a few weeks.

Several weeks went by and I still hadn't heard anything from EAS. Finally, while driving a young client of mine to his tennis lesson, my pager buzzed. I looked at the number and recognized it was a Colorado area code. I said to my client, "We need to go back to your house and have your mom call this phone number."

His mother called, and after a brief pause, she relayed this message, "Yes, this is Bill Phillips. I have my brother Shawn and the entire EAS staff in my office. We all would like to congratulate Brad and ask him what color Corvette he would like."

Upon hearing the news that I'd won, we all jumped up and down like kids on Christmas morning. I had achieved another dream. A few days later, Phillips sent me a fax in which he stated that he would travel to Orlando by the end of the week to present me the new car at the Disney Yacht Club. I could hardly wait. I called my parents and my brother who all joined with me in celebration.

The day I received the car, I drove by myself to Disney World in my Honda Civic. When I saw Phillips, after a quick greeting, I excitedly blurted, "Where's the 'vette?"

He pointed and said, grinning, "Over there."

And there it sat. A beautiful black on black Corvette. Phillips took time to go over the features of the car, the start button, and the six-speed transmission. Then he took me for a test drive through the back roads of the Disney World complex. I barely had my seatbelt locked in when he peeled out. At first I was a little concerned he was wearing out the rubber on my new tires. He drove like we were at the Daytona Speedway. But it was all good fun.

Later that day Phillips and his girlfriend were kind enough to drive my Honda Civic while I drove the Corvette to the Miss Galaxy contest at Disney which featured over a hundred female fitness models.

Phillips is a great guy who cares about people and improving our nation's health. After the Miss Galaxy competition, Phillips, his girlfriend, and I met for some fun at the theme parks. At one of the games, Phillips offered me a $100 if I could ring the bell by slamming the mallet. "Sure I'll give it a try." I swung the mallet, rang the bell and out came Phillips' wallet as he handed me a brand new hundred dollar bill. I asked if he wanted me to do it again. He laughed.

After the contest and spending the evening with Phillips and Cusack, while driving my new car home I got hungry so I pulled into a Subway near one of the exits off Interstate 4. While the guys made my sub, I said, "Guys, guys, guess what? I just won a Corvette and $50,000. That one out there in the parking lot." Because I didn't know a lot of people in Orlando at the time, those workers were the first who heard about my winnings.

I kept that car for the duration of the four-year contract and then I sold it. I didn't drive it much. It's a high-maintenance car, very expensive. My dad is a finance guy and he encouraged me to sell it and invest the money. So that's what I did.

My next big break in my modeling career started when my agent lined up an audition in Orlando for the NordicFlex ad campaign. A few years earlier I had auditioned for a similar job with Soloflex in which I drove four hours to Miami for a morning audition. At least a hundred models, all in top shape, showed up that day. After showing my portfolio and doing a few poses for my audition, I thought I didn't have a chance so I drove back to Orlando.

Surprisingly the next day I was one of the top ten to receive a call-back. I drove back to Miami for a second audition. After sixteen hours of driving I found out I didn't get the job. Remembering the disappointment of the Soloflex job, I wanted to make the most of my opportunity with NordicFlex, so I spent the week in  preparation cutting up. I ate a low fat, high protein diet and increased my cardio, to make sure my abs were razor sharp. The NordicFlex audition went well. A few days later, my agent paged me to say I had landed the job.

I found out they wanted me to be a swimmer in this ad. For weeks before the shoot I practiced my flip turns at the nearby Lake Brantley swimming pool and became pretty good at it. However, when I got to Portland, Oregon, for the shoot, a rep informed me they had decided to use me as a runner instead. The photo shoot took place in someone's home overlooking beautiful downtown Portland. Tracks for the cameras, big stage lighting, and motion picture cameras were set up all over the place for use by the large crew. I thought we might film a major motion picture. A smorgasbord of healthy food was available to eat too.

I spent hours running across the Portland Bridge and on set demonstrating the exercises with their equipment for their nationally televised ad campaign. The director happened to see some of my portfolio pictures during a break, and decided he wanted to use me on the cover of their mailing campaign, which was called "Perfected."

At the time, I felt perfected. I had grown from a skinny 100-pound weakling with hearing aids dangling from my ears into a world tennis champion and EAS bodybuilding champion who was gaining recognition at places where I least expected it. At the airport coming home from Portland, while getting a sandwich from the deli, the gentleman behind the counter asked if I was the guy from *Muscle Media*.

"That's right," I said and tossed him a pack of Myoplex protein.

When NordicFlex hit the airwaves and the malls, friends and family called to say they saw me running on television.

I am thankful and enjoyed receiving the recognition and accolades as I continued modeling and teaching tennis, but deep down inside, something was still missing.

With High School Coach Reidmeyer and Doubles Partner Jeff Parrish

Highland Elementary A Team – Coach Dad on Left
(I'm third from the right, second row)

Finale and Bow after Toledo Fashion Show

Struttin' On The Cat Walk

Wearing Denim (second from right) on International Drive Billboard

101

PTR Player of the Year Award with
Dennis Van der Meer

Teaching the audience how
the deaf applaud

Carrying the Flag at the Opening Ceremonies
for the Dresse Cup in Bradenton, Florida

Sharing Dresse Cup victory with
Mom and Dad

My two best buddies, Dad and brother Jim

My two favorite girls, my wife Ginny and my Mom

In Tennis you meet people
from everywhere

Team USA having fun in
Copenhagen

Beautiful Copenhagen!

Bless My Speech Therapist! At a speaking engagement

Teaching tennis to some of my favorite people – Kids!

The First & Second EAS Champions

Body For Life founder,
Bill Phillips, shining my
new Corvette

2nd EAS
Bodybuilding
Champion

106

Our Wedding Day Was a Gift From God

Our tennis loving
assistant coach,
Honeybear

Ginny and I doing what we love best –
Serving the Lord on the tennis court at
an FCA Boys Camp

"Run in such a way as to get the prize."
1 Corinthians 9:24

Chapter 8 | Born Again

I love telling the story of how I met Jesus. In fact, it's my favorite story about my life. Despite all the modeling, tennis, and bodybuilding successes, something was missing. I couldn't put my finger on it. I couldn't tell if the feeling was some sort of unrest or a "is this all there is" attitude. I thought what more could I want? I've got a job, recognition, a nice car—just about everything a person could want. But I was wrong.

After I had become the second EAS spokesperson, I started feeling a lot of anxiety, stress, and pressure inside. Friends and acquaintances didn't know anything was wrong. To them, everything looked bright and rosy. After all, when they looked at me they saw a man who had achieved many of his goals and dreams while overcoming adversity. To them, I was a huge success in life.

But inside I was hurting pretty badly. My girlfriend and I had broken up after a brief engagement. We had dated for eight years and it seemed right to move onto a more serious commitment. However, soon after we got engaged, I decided I wanted time to myself. So I suggested to my fiancée that she go live with her family in New Jersey. She didn't like the idea, but agreed. Our engagement ended within three months after she moved when we mutually called it off. I flew up to get the ring and to have closure. I was heartbroken. I felt like someone had shoved a knife through my heart. I'd never felt so alone.

My family said I could move back to Ohio if I wanted. There, I'd have had the security of family, friends, relatives and familiar surroundings. But I told them I wanted to ride out the storm in the Orlando area. I cried myself to sleep many nights.

While all of this was going on—the breakup, the traveling to promote EAS—I was training a friend. We met at a local gym a couple days a week. He often talked to me about the Bible and important things that he'd read since we last worked out. Of course, I'd heard about the Bible. Who hasn't, right? I had a Bible, but it was home on a bookshelf collecting dust. If someone had pressed me for an answer I couldn't have told them the last time I'd read it.

He encouraged me to read. Each time, I thought, "What? Read the Bible? Why should I do that?" What could it possibly have to offer me? At the time I couldn't see myself as the Bible reading type. I liked to have fun, chew tobacco, and do my thing.

When we met to workout he'd ask if I had read anything during the past week. When I told him no, he still encouraged me to do so. With a gnawing feeling growing, I relented one night while alone in my apartment. I pulled my Bible from the shelf, blew off the dust, and opened it to a verse he had mentioned that day. For the next few days, I read my Bible. But the stories seemed meaningless and long. I often wondered how something written thousands of years ago would have any impact or bearing on my life today. I wasn't really able to understand anything so I quit reading.

The anxiety and guilt mounted. My mind didn't understand the words I had been reading, but my spirit did as they began to plow up the fallow ground of my heart. Not long after my fiancée and I ended our relationship, I felt overwhelmed with anxiety. I pulled into a Walmart parking lot to take some deep breaths. My heart raced as I gasped for air. I stayed in the parking lot, with the car idling, for quite a while taking long, deep breaths. All sorts of crazy things ran through my head. I struggled to get my breathing and mind in order. I thought I might be losing my mind. I trembled and broke out in a cold sweat. When I calmed down, I went home to my apartment, and tried to do the things that normally made me feel good. I played tennis, lifted weights, drank beer, and soaked in the hot bathtub. No matter what I did, the nagging feeling wouldn't stop. I was tempted to pack my bags and head back home to Ohio, but I was determined to stay in Florida and weather the storm, no pun intended.

After we finished my Christian client's next workout, I motioned for him to join me outside. I explained what was going on with me. He listened intently, never saying a word. He listened. Before he said a word, he took a sip of his protein shake, closed the lid until it snapped, smiled and then slowly turned around so I could read the back of his T-shirt. It read: "Here I am. I stand at the door and knock. If anyone hears my voice and opens the door, I will come in and eat with that person, and they with me. To the one who is victorious, I will give the right to sit with me on my throne, just as I was victorious and sat down with my Father on his throne. Whoever has ears, let them hear what the Spirit says to the churches."

The scripture is Revelation 3:20-22 and the verses rang loud and clear like nothing else ever had before. At that moment, I knew God was speaking to me. And my moment of truth stood right before me. More importantly, I had to decide what to do next. I had two options: head back inside to the gym or listen to my friend as he turned to face me. My friend explained we are all in need of a Savior because of our sinful nature.

We read in Romans 3:23, "For all have sinned and fallen short of the glory of God." And in Romans 6:23, "The wages of sin is death."

There are many verses in the Bible regarding salvation, such as John 3:3: "Jesus replied, "Very truly I tell you, no one can see the kingdom of God unless they are born again." Probably two of the most well-known verses are John 3:16-17, "For God so loved the world that he gave his one and only Son, that whoever believes in him shall not perish but have eternal life. For God did not send his Son into the world to condemn the world, but to save the world through him."

Without knowing those verses at that moment, God made me realize I was guilty of sins punishable by death. The realization of how much I had lived in sin all my life hit me like the proverbial 2x4 in the face. But God sent His son to save me, to give me—and others who believe and accept Jesus as the way—eternal salvation.

By now, we had settled into his car. As I sat in the passenger's seat, he asked, "Brad, are you ready to ask Jesus Christ into your heart and make him your Lord and Savior?"

Trying to hold back tears, I mumbled a very weak, "Yes. I am."

He laid his hand on my shoulder and asked me to pray after him. The prayer went something like this: "Heavenly Father, I respond to your invitation and come to you in the name of your son Jesus Christ. I come with all my sins, heartaches, and addictions. I turn away from the evil of my past life and turn to you Lord Jesus. I believe that you died for my sin and that you rose from the dead. You are the son of the Living God. By faith, I receive forgiveness and your free gift of salvation. Thank you for accepting me as your child. Fill me with the power of your Holy Spirit, so that I may follow you all the days of my life. I believe in my heart what I now confess with my mouth; Jesus is my savior, my Lord and my God. I pray for this in the name of Jesus."

While we prayed, I cried hard, very hard. Gym members walked by the car as we prayed and peeked in the car to see what was going on. I didn't care. I knew the God of the universe was speaking to my heart. After we prayed, it felt as if all the pressure, stress, guilt, anxiety, despair, and everything that hurt were lifted off my shoulders. Anyone who has experienced this knows what I'm talking about. If you haven't, consider accepting Jesus into your life. Make him your Lord and Savior.

The presence of the Holy Spirit overwhelmed me too. It was an incredible, powerful feeling. I moved from being unworthy and lost to a wonderful place of peace that felt glorious.

Sometime later I read Romans 11:33-36 and was reminded of the feeling I experienced that day. It says, "Oh, the depth of the riches of the wisdom and knowledge of God. How unsearchable his judgments, and his paths beyond tracing out. Who has known the mind of the Lord? Or who has been his counselor? Who has ever given to God, that God should repay them? For from him and through him and for him are all things. To him be the glory forever. Amen."

I don't mean to sound preachy at this point, but you have to understand where I came from, what I had overcome, to get to this point in my life.

I started reading the Bible again. This time things made sense. My spiritual eyes had been opened and the Bible came to life for me. This might sound strange to someone who has never read the Bible or become born again. The things I didn't understand, I wasn't afraid to ask my friend for help. For the first time in my life, I looked forward to reading the Bible, and I still do to this day, nearly twenty years after saying that prayer of salvation. There is incredible wisdom and much we can learn from God's word.

You probably can tell by now I don't do anything half-hearted. I put everything into my pursuits. Now, instead of pursuing earthly gain, I was in hot pursuit of knowledge of and a relationship with my Lord and Savior.

Romans 10:11-13 says, "Anyone who believes in him will never be put to shame. For there is no difference between Jew and Gentile—the same Lord is Lord of all and richly blesses all who call on him, for, Everyone who calls on the name of the Lord will be saved."

Now that my spirit man was alive to the words I read in the Bible, I began to see God in everything around me. Something I never really thought about before. I noticed things that reminded me of a verse I had just read, and God somehow made those words come to life for me. I discovered this book that is thousands of years old does apply to my life today. The more I read the Bible, the more faith I had and the stronger I felt. Not physically, but spiritually which carried over into other aspects of my life. Before that salvation prayer I relied too much on self-confidence to get me through difficult situations, where now I have Christ-confidence.

Being named EAS spokesman and winning the $50,000 couldn't have come at a better time. Each month I received a check for a little more than $1,000 and all the protein shakes and supplements I wanted. This allowed me to spend almost an entire year reading the Bible. I spent time in my room getting to know Jesus better. I prayed and talked to God—a lot. I no longer had the desire to do anything but to learn more about God's word and to know

God better through his word. I have learned God's ways are much different than man's ways.

The Bible says in Matthew 6:33 that we should "seek first His kingdom and His righteousness, and all these things will be given to you as well."

Until I was born again, Corvettes, money, prestige, and success were the most important things in my life. I thought being in magazines and receiving recognition for success like that would make me feel better about myself and in turn allow me to help others feel good about themselves. Those material things were only temporary help. They may have opened doors, but I didn't have any substance to pour into others. Now I do, with the grace and blessings of Christ.

What a wonderful God we serve. Everything lives by His power, and everything for His glory. Everything I'd accomplished paled in comparison to my new life in Christ.

Now I share every day that only through Jesus Christ can we experience what really matters in life: love, peace, joy, patience, and kindness.

"Prayer is the exercise of drawing on the grace of God."
Oswald Chambers

Chapter 9 | Power of Prayer

I spent the first thirty years of my life building my physical man and my self-confidence. While focusing on that I neglected the spirit man. 1 Timothy 4:8 says, "For physical training has some value, but spiritual training is of far greater value, for it has benefits not only in this life but the life to come."

After being born again, with the monthly checks from EAS providing financial support, I spent a lot of time in God's word and in prayer. At first I didn't pray well. I stumbled over words I thought I should pray. I struggled with what to say sometimes. Like many new believers, I put a lot of pressure on myself to say the right thing to God. Nor was I comfortable praying out loud in front of others, but I soon realized He isn't as concerned with the words as we are. He looks into our hearts to see our intention.

1 Samuel 16:7 says, "... The Lord does not look at the things people look at. People look at the outward appearance, but the Lord looks at the heart."

During that year I went from a newbie who struggled to say the right words to a more confident man who prayed diligently and without ceasing. The more I prayed, the better I got, at least I think I did, particularly when God started answering some of those prayers. For example, I had developed a bad habit of chewing tobacco. I knew it wasn't good for me because I am a personal trainer teaching others to walk in good health. I tried hard on my own to quit. I would go to the gas station, buy a can of tobacco, put in a dip, feel guilty, and then throw away the can. The next day, craving a dip, I would repeat the same action. One night while on my bed I cried out to God, "Lord, I know this isn't good for me and I know this isn't your will, please help me to stop." And I haven't had a dip since.

Another answered prayer was improved language. While casually hanging out with friends I learned everything I spoke mattered and when I said a swear word or told a dirty joke I felt conviction from the Holy Spirit and was quick to repent. Over time my language improved and I learned to avoid questionable conversations. This allowed me to grow stronger in my walk with the Lord.

About two years after giving my life to the Lord I was lonely. I'd recently ended a two-year relationship with a woman who lived in the same apartment complex as me. I knew I was still an infant Christian and had a lot of growing to do. The first thing I desired in a wife was someone who loved the Lord like I did and who would help me to grow spiritually. The Bible tells us that if we pray and ask the Lord for anything according to His will, He will give it to us. It was 1998, I was in my early thirties and thought I should settle down. So I prayed for a wife every day.

But I was missing a key component. The friend who had led me to the Lord said I needed to be *specific* in my prayer. I could do that, and I changed my prayer to ask the Lord to show me my wife by the end of the year.

By the time September rolled around, I wondered when I would meet my wife. Some people thought I wasn't giving myself much of a chance because I didn't frequent nightclubs and other places where many people look for a wife. Instead, I stayed in my bedroom to seek the Lord's guidance through prayer and reading the Bible. I decided to trust God and not worry about it.

Early one September day at the park where I taught tennis in Orlando, the front desk lady informed me a wonderful single Christian girl would be in my class. With eight tennis pros at this park, it was a miracle she ended up on my court for a lesson.

Ginny was a skinny blonde with gorgeous eyes, nice legs, and warm personality. She impressed me with her on-court speed and love of the game. She would stay for hours after our lessons to hit with other students. We got to know each other a little bit each week at the courts and finally one Saturday after clinic I decided to invite her to church with me and she said yes. She was thrilled to go.

She continued her weekly lessons and our friendship grew during my tennis clinics and attending church together on Sundays. One day after Saturday lessons, I returned to the court where she was practicing her serves. I asked if she wanted to come over for a pizza and watch football. Instead of going back inside and onto the court, I spoke to her through the green wind screen that covered the chain-link fence around the courts. I discovered this was a big mistake. I wasn't sure whether she said yes or no because I couldn't read her lips. I motioned her over to the viewing area and asked again. She said yes and smiled, adding she'd love to.

As was my regular routine, I went to the gym that afternoon. While working out, I ran into Paul, a friend of mine from church. He told me about the community service work he had been doing at the homeless shelter. He asked if I wanted to join him. I wanted to, but said I had a date. I told him I'd ask if she wanted to join us. When I asked, Ginny said she'd be happy to do it. I served mashed potatoes; Ginny poured the lemonade. Several others volunteered as well. Hundreds of people showed up that night for food.

When we finished around 8:00 p.m., I asked if she still wanted to come over for a movie and pizza. When she agreed, we ordered the pizza and rented a movie, however we also had to make a quick stop at Walmart to buy a VCR because I didn't own one. We ate dinner and watched *Zorro*. Well, I watched part of it. Exhausted from teaching tennis all morning, lifting weights, and feeding the homeless, I fell asleep on the sofa. I woke up to see Ginny putting on her shoes. I apologized and Ginny laughed before we said good night.

After a few months of dating, I realized Ginny was special and much different than most other girls I'd met. If a movie had too much violence or foul language, she would leave. She wouldn't spend the night either. That was new to me too. The only time she did stay—and slept on the couch—was the time a major hurricane came through Central Florida.

Some of the many things that attracted me to Ginny were her knowledge of the Bible from her attending Rhema Bible College in Tulsa, Oklahoma, she attended church, is an overcomer, and, most of all, she loved Jesus. As we got to know each other, I saw incredible strength in her character.

Ginny had been sexually assaulted at gunpoint her senior year in high school and her first husband was unfaithful. Yet, she has a strong relationship with Jesus who gave her the strength to forgive and press on while keeping a tender heart.

I thought this is the kind of woman I wanted to grow old with. Despite being a new Christian with some rough edges, I understood the need to be with a strong partner with similar beliefs and values. God created marriage, and I believe it's important each person has a strong personal relationship with Jesus Christ before making that lifetime commitment. If both actively seek Jesus, the relationship with the Lord and each other will grow.

We started dating casually in October 1998. By Christmas we were serious. After about nine months of dating and praying about it, I believed Ginny was the woman God wanted me to marry. When I received that answer, I prayed for God to show me a great way to propose. A few days later He revealed His plan while I worked out at World Gym, the same place I was led to the

Lord. That day, I bumped into David, a friend I'd modeled with years before at a Nike fashion show. While we talked, David said he was Indiana Jones in a show in which actors perform parts of the movie on stage for a live audience at nearby Disney-MGM Studios, now Hollywood Studios. We talked a little bit more before going off to finish our workouts. After completing a set of bicep curls, I wandered over and asked if we could work something out so I could propose to Ginny at the show. He nodded and said, "We probably could work something out for you."

Alright, I was excited about the proposal. David asked me to contact him after giving him time to check with the studio. When I did, we set up a lunch meeting and discussed a date for me to propose. However, we didn't discuss the actual plan. When the day was set, I checked the weather forecast: rain was on the way. My heart sank. And sure enough it rained. I shouldn't have been surprised. It rains often in Florida in September and October.

Rain washed out attempts the following two Fridays as well. Now, almost a month later, we had a Friday with no rain in the forecast so I called David to iron out the details. He told me the bad news of his leg injury that would keep him from performing that week. I couldn't believe it. I knew God wanted me to marry Ginny, but things weren't working out for the perfect proposal. It's now four weeks after the original date, and I still hadn't proposed yet.

Then I did what most guys would do, I took matters into my own hands. I decided to ask Ginny to marry me during one of our regular walks around the Post Lake Apartment complex where I lived. The plan was to sit in the swing set on one side of the lake, a place where no one sat most of the time when I walked by. But that day, someone did. With the ring in my pocket, we kept walking and sat in the next swing set. At last, we're sitting, but palmetto bushes and a big tree blocked our view of the lake. I was about to pop the question when Ginny said the view wasn't very good and she wanted to leave. At this point, I wondered if I'd ever get a chance to ask this woman to marry me. I almost gave her the ring anyway because I didn't know how much longer I could wait.

But I decided not to give up on the proposal plan at MGM and contacted David one more time. I asked David if we could do it the following Friday. I looked at the weather report for Friday, October 22, 1999. All clear. The big day had finally arrived, but the obstacles weren't over yet.

Ginny, who didn't have a clue I was planning to propose because we hadn't discussed marriage, took the day off from work. We ate a delicious breakfast at the Longwood First Watch, a popular eatery in the Orlando area, and headed to MGM Studios.

It was a perfect fall day with clear blue skies, cool and crisp with no humidity. While I drove, Ginny found a note in my truck written by one of my female clients. She was a little upset when she read the note and saw it was signed with a "pet name." After we cleared up that misunderstanding, I received a page from my boss telling me that I had tennis lessons that morning I needed to cover.

When we arrived at MGM, we contacted my boss and cleared up the situation. Ironically, we parked in the "Romance" section at the park.

I was still not sure how the whole thing would pan out because David and I never finalized the details of my role in the show and how I would pop the question. Nonetheless, I did my best to hide my nervousness. I knew everything was in God's hands, but I couldn't wait to see how it all worked out.

David had asked me to meet him at the 1:30 p.m. show for further instructions. Ginny couldn't understand why we had to wait for a later show since we were running out of things to see and do. But I was able to hold her off. To stall I ate a big turkey leg for about forty-five minutes then we arrived at the Indiana Jones show in plenty of time and sat near the front. I looked for David but couldn't find him. I then noticed people on the stage were whispering to each other. Finally, the stage director made an announcement: "That due to technical difficulties, we have to cancel the show. Please come back for the next show."

Not another delay, I thought. We walked toward the left exit. At the top of the stadium, we ran into David. I did my best to act surprised to see him. After introducing David to Ginny, I asked, "What are you doing here?"

He said, "I work here at the show and I'm here to pick up my paycheck."

Ginny chimed in excitedly, saying I wanted to play one of the extras in the show. Earlier in the day, I told her about the time my cousin, mom and dad and I were extras in the A-Team show at the Los Angeles MGM Studios. David said he could probably get me in it. I knew all of this, but played along. I may have been cool on the outside, but inside I was nervous. I struggled to picture the details of the proposal, what I would say, and if I would hear the necessary instructions. When the gates opened for the next show, David led us down to the second row, front and center. While we sat, I bounced my knees like a piston in a race car. Oh man, I wanted to do this, but what was I going to say when that moment arrived? Would I hear them call my name to go on stage?

Before the show began, a lady came out to ask for six volunteers. She asked for a "brave and patient person." I didn't hear what she said so David told me to raise my hand. Of course, she picked me. When they selected all the volunteers, she led us backstage for a quick costume change. We returned to the stage wearing Middle Eastern costumes. The director joined us to go over a few details. He chose me to re-enact a shooting scene. I was to pull a fake knife and charge him. Then he shot me. I dropped to the ground, faking a death in a way that would make any veteran Hollywood actor proud. Then I stood and the director said, "That was very good, Brad. Now, is there anything else you would like to say?"

He thrust the microphone into my hand, catching me off-guard in front of a packed auditorium. It took me a second to realize what was happening. My time had come to propose.

I said, "Yes, my name is Brad Minns and I'm not an actor, but my love for this woman is very real. She's sitting right over there and her name is Ginny Hall."

Ginny's eyes widened and her mouth opened slightly. David had to nudge her to join me on stage. I got down on one knee, with the ring in my hand, and said, "Ginny, I love you very much, will you marry me?"

With tears in our eyes, she said, "Yes! With all my heart," and bent down to hug me.

Applause broke out all over the auditorium. Cast members congratulated us. I left to sit with Ginny, but the

director called me back to the stage to finish the show. Ginny sat with the ring in the box on her lap, smiling the whole time. After the show we walked through the park, and people who had attended that show came up and gave us their best wishes and congratulations. It was a day we will never forget.

As you can see, God does answer prayers. He did mine—in a big way. And in His time, not ours. I not only had to wait on Him revealing my wife. I also had to wait, for the right time, to propose.

God's timing is always perfect. Because of this answered prayer and momentous occasion, Ginny and I like to celebrate God's goodness every year, not only on our wedding anniversary, but also the day we got engaged. This was a landmark moment in our lives.

The following is an email Ginny sent to her co-workers after our engagement:

"Guess Who's Getting Married?"

Brad proposed on Friday, October 22nd, 1999. Let

me tell you all the wonderful story... He had been wanting to take me to MGM Studios for several weeks, but the weather was so rainy, we didn't go. On Friday, we were finally able to go, the weather was absolutely perfect.

We went to the Indiana Jones show at 1:30, and towards

the end, they stopped the show and said that "due to technical difficulties, they had to cancel the show and please come back for the 2:45 show". As Brad and I were leaving, he ran into a friend of his (David) that just happened to work there as Indiana Jones in the show, but he had the day off and stopped by to pick something up. I told David that Brad was talking about being one of the volunteers they pick out of the audience to play an extra in the show. He said no problem and he could probably get Brad in it. So he walks us down to a reserved 2nd row from the front. When the lady was asking for volunteers, David told Brad to raise his hand when she asked for a man who was "brave and patient". Sure enough, she picked Brad. He went off stage with the other six or so volunteers for wardrobe, and came back dressed in a turban and tunic like they were in the Middle East. Then afterwards they had to act out different things the director wanted them to do, he chose Brad to do the death scene. Brad had to walk towards him like he had a knife and the man shot him and Brad plopped down on the ground like he was dead. Then he stood up, and the director said "that was very good Brad, is there anything else you would like to say?" He *gave Brad the microphone (in front of a packed stadium) and he said "Yes, my name is Brad Minns, and I'm not an actor, but my love for this woman is very real, she's sitting right over there and her name is Ginny Hall." I was frozen in my seat. David, who was sitting next to me, said "get up Ginny, go down front" so I walked down to the stage, and Brad got down on his knee and with a ring in his hand, said, "Ginny, I love you very much, will you marry me? And we both had tears in our eyes. Of course I said "yes, with all my heart." Everyone in the whole place clapped for us, and for the rest of the day throughout the park, people kept telling us "congratulations" because they had seen the show... I have never been so surprised in my whole life. The whole cast and crew were in on it... Brad and David had planned it for the last month. We are planning to be married on Easter Sunday, April 23rd, 2000, in Leu Gardens. God doesn't always answer our prayers when we want Him to ... but it's always worth the wait when he does.*

"Marriage is love personified."
Unknown

Chapter 10 | Paradise at Last

Ginny and I planned to get married six months from our engagement date, which put the date at April 22, 2000. After asking everyone we knew where to have a wedding, the general consensus seemed to be Leu Gardens. Neither of us had been there before, but Ginny called to check on the availability for our desired date. The wedding receptionist explained it was necessary to book Leu Gardens a year in advance. She paused and explained they had just received a cancellation for the following day, April 23, 2000, Easter Sunday. The rose garden was booked on a first-come, first-serve basis, so we asked her to hold the date for their three-day holding period while we checked out the place.

Ginny and I decided to meet at Leu Gardens during her lunch break. She got there first and emailed me: "Brad, you've got to come and see this place. It's absolutely gorgeous."

Before I got out of the car, I knew this would be the perfect place for an outdoor Southern wedding just by the sights and aromas of the property. We met with the wedding planner and took a grand tour of the beautiful grounds along the winding sidewalks lined with moss-covered oaks and blooming camellias, which led to the incredible rose garden, the site of the wedding ceremony. We said in unison, "We'll take it."

Easter Sunday is a special day for Ginny because that was the day she gave her life to the Lord her senior year in high school.

After we reserved the place for our wedding, we went to work selecting the photographer, caterer, florist, invitations, and all the other details involved in planning a wedding. I found the photographer and Ginny pretty much did the rest. Mom flew Ginny up to Toledo and hosted a bridal shower for her at the Highland Meadows Country Club, home of the Jamie Farr Golf Classic. Ginny was able to meet a lot of friends and family, and everyone had a great time. Later, my Dad flew to Orlando to attend a wedding shower three of my clients hosted for us. It was a grand time and everyone was excited about April 23 that rapidly approached.

What made all of this so special was the incredible generosity of our friends and family who were all supportive of our decision to make this lifelong commitment to each other.

One thing that made me a little nervous, and had been for years, was the thought, "Will I be able to understand the pastor and recite the wedding vows properly?" We made the decision to ask the associate pastor from our church, Pastor Orlando, to officiate the wedding. Everything was coming together beautifully.

The hotel we selected for our out of town friends and relatives was right around the corner from Virginia

Drive. We celebrated my brother Jim's birthday at the hotel on the eve of our wedding, and shared good food, drink, laughter and stories with one another in anticipation of a beautiful wedding the next day.

Easter Sunday, April 23, 2000, couldn't have been more perfect. Without a cloud in the sky, the sun beat down on us unobstructed. Guests and family enjoyed a buffet breakfast at the hotel while Ginny was at her apartment getting ready for the big day. I explained to Pastor Orlando how important it was for me to be able to read his lips during the ceremony and I had been concerned about this moment ever since I was a young man. He assured me not to worry and everything would work out. Boy was he ever right.

When everyone was seated in the rose garden, the harpist began playing her music while I stood with Pastor Orlando, the bridesmaids, and groomsmen. We waited patiently for the bride. Then ... I saw Ginny. My heart raced. My beautiful bride entered the rose garden escorted

by her father. Struggling to hold back the tears, I did my best to look like I had it all together. As I stood there I realized that finding a wife and making a commitment for life is one of the most glorious gifts and decisions a man can make. I remembered the Bible verse that says, "He who finds a wife finds what is good and receives favor from the Lord" (Prov. 18:22).

Much to my relief, Pastor Orlando stood by Ginny's left shoulder where I could see them both at the same time. As we recited our wedding vows, I paused to hold back the tears. Later Ginny jokingly told me she thought I was changing my mind. I was thanking God for his incredible blessing.

Pastor Orlando's message was divinely inspired.

Ginny and I don't remember the entire sermon, but we do recall the theme centered on salvation. His message must have resonated because we heard soon after several people made a decision for Christ and several friends who were living together decided to get married.

I made it through reciting our vows without any mistakes and Ginny looked bold and confident as a lion. After we finished, everyone headed to the reception at the top of the hill in the beautiful lake view Southern mansion. Finally, Ginny and I were able to put our newly acquired dancing skills to use. All the moves I learned went down the drain and Ginny and I held onto each other and did the "Fonzie" dance in which the guy pulls his girl close and rocks back and forth. But in our minds it was a beautiful waltz.

After a fun time of dinner and dancing, Jim gave the wedding toast and did an incredible job for which we are very grateful. I will always  remember what he said about me: "Brad is a fighter." Ginny's mom still talks about his inspiring toast.

Up to this point, we had all the bases covered for a perfect wedding, yet I wasn't sure if my red pickup truck  would be waiting for us outside. I was relieved when the doors opened and we ran through the shower of rice to see parked out front a new black window tinted town car that had been arranged by our dear friend, Linda. Inside the car was a silver bucket of ice-cold champagne, and two dinner plates. When I asked our chauffer his name, guess what his response was? "My name is Angel." he said. Here I am getting married in Orlando, by Pastor Orlando, marrying Virginia on Virginia Drive, and being escorted to our honeymoon by a guy named Angel. All I could think was "Wow!"

We spent the night at the airport Hyatt hotel because of our early flight to St. Thomas, Virgin Islands the next morning. Our flight was like a scene out of a movie. We flew over the beautiful blue ocean and all of a sudden mountains appeared out of nowhere. After a quick stop in Puerto Rico, we arrived at our destination in about two hours. We checked into our room which overlooked Magens Bay Beach, at the time considered one of the top ten  beaches in the world. We had never seen water so clear and blue. The seafood, snorkeling, horseback riding and sightseeing were second to none. My first morning after about ten minutes in the gym, I told myself "What am I doing in the gym?" From that moment on, Ginny and I enjoyed buttered toast each morning for our poolside breakfasts with breathtaking views of the ocean. Most nights, we ate the biggest lobster I've ever seen, except for one night when we decided to order pizza, which took about two hours for the delivery, but no free pizza.

When it came time to return to home, we called our friend Linda to find out if we had a ride and she assured us it was all taken care of. Upon arriving at Orlando International Airport and coming down the escalator, much to our delight, there stood a driver greeting us with a sign welcoming Mr. and Mrs. Minns. I liked the sound of that, Mr. and Mrs. Minns. No longer would I introduce Ginny as my girlfriend, but as my wife.

We both believe marriage was created by God and it is for life. For richer, for poorer, in sickness and health, and good times and not so good. With Christ at the helm, we believe He will see us through each day and draw us closer to Him and to one another. Mark 10:9 says, "Therefore what God has joined together, let man not separate."

"It is more blessed to give than to receive."
Acts 20:35

Chapter 11 | Giving Back

It has become my family's Christmas tradition to enjoy the Charles Dickens classic *Scrooge* starring Albert Finney. As many of you know, the story is about a hard-hearted miser who is obsessed with money and has little time for anyone or anything else. After being visited by three spirits in his dreams he awakens to sorrowful repentance and decides to turn his life around by giving away all his treasured possessions. This shocked everyone in town and filled them with joy and happiness, and turned Scrooge's life around for the good.

Matthew 6:21 says, "For where your treasure is, there your heart will be also."

In 2005, twenty years after I had won the Gold medal in L.A., I heard a message at church that spoke to my heart about being thankful. While sharing on giving back, the pastor said, "It is not about selfish ambition and personal gain. It's about what you can do for others."

At that moment I felt God was reminding me of all the people who had helped me to accomplish my dreams in my life. I have been blessed with a great family, as well as friends, neighbors, teachers, and coaches who went the extra mile to help me to succeed. Without them, I cannot imagine where I would be.

Later that week I sat in my recliner in the living room of our apartment and skimmed through the 1985 yearbook for the World Games for the Deaf that I had recently received in the mail. I thought about how Bill Austin and his team at Starkey Labs had sponsored me and Team USA. Not only that, Starkey had set up shop in L.A. and fitted deaf athletes from the U.S. and other countries with the company's newest, top-of-the-line hearing aids. Starkey also gave free hearing tests to the athletes, as well as anyone else who wanted one.

As I flipped through the yearbook, the words from my pastor kept running through my mind: "It's about what you can do for others."

Austin, founder and CEO of Starkey, came to mind. I wondered if I ever thanked him for the awesome experience of participating 1985 World Games when I won the Gold medal. Starkey had done a lot for us. But that was twenty years ago and I honestly couldn't remember if I had thanked him. I hoped that I had.

The mission of Starkey, the world's leading manufacturer of custom hearing instruments with more than one million customers, was, and still is, to bring understanding among people through hearing care by focusing on awareness, education, protection and treatment, so the world may hear. According to the company's website, "From Day 1, Starkey has operated under the single-minded purpose that 'Hearing is our concern.'" I know without Starkey's sponsorship and hearing aids, I not only wouldn't have been able to participate in the 1985

Games, but I also wouldn't enjoy the communication and understanding in the things I love to do. In many ways, I owed Austin and his company a deep gratitude of thanks. His hearing aids have been a blessing to me and have allowed me to enjoy the gift of hearing.

I decided to send a brief thank you email to Starkey, which appears below.

Dear Mr. Austin,

This afternoon I came upon the 1985 World Games for the Deaf yearbook. I know this may be a bit late but I wanted to take a moment to express my deepest thanks and appreciation for all of Starkey's support in helping not only myself but the entire United States Deaf Olympic Team in our quest for the gold at the Los Angeles World Games for the Deaf.

I appreciate your generosity now more than ever. The memories have stayed with me all of these years and I'll never forget when I participated and won the men's tennis competition defeating the defending champion Jeff Osbourne in a 5 set come from behind win. I keep a framed photo from Starkey in our gym of that match as a reminder that no matter what the score is in tennis or life that you should never give up.

Thanks again for everything.
Sincerely,
Brad Minns

The following day I received an unexpected email from Bill's wife, Tani Austin, asking if I wanted to thank Austin in person at the annual Gala in Minnesota the next weekend, August 20. I gladly accepted and began to pray about what I should give Austin as a "thank you" gift.

Because I'd never attended in person, I didn't know the Gala is a huge event. Each year the Gala is held to raise money to send missions teams around the world to give the gift of hearing to those in need. The year Ginny and I attended, country singer Trisha Yearwood, and pop singers Michael Bolton and Donny Osmond entertained the crowd. Garth Brooks also was in attendance, as well as Lorraine Bracco, Robert Culp, Lou Ferrigno, Senator John Glenn, Marlee Matlin, Leslie Nielsen, Mickey Rooney, Marion Ross, and Paul Michaels. A then-record $4-plus million was raised for the Starkey Hearing Foundation.

In 2012, a record $7.6 million was raised with former President Bill Clinton, and comedians Robin Williams, Billy Crystal and Chevy Chase in attendance.

I didn't have to wait long for an answer to my prayer. It came, like they most often do, in a quiet thought from the Holy Spirit: "Give him the Gold medal."

Okay, now that I had my marching orders, I needed to get the medal from my mom and dad's new home in Michigan. When Mom answered my call, I didn't give her much of a chance to greet me before I blurted, "Mom, I'm going to give Bill Austin my Gold medal. Can you send it to me so I can frame it?"

Her response was a brief cause for concern. "Oh, I don't know dear," she said. "We just moved into our new home and it's probably not unpacked yet."

I asked Mom to have my brother Jim look for it. I stressed that I needed it in the next two days so I'd have time to get it framed. Ginny and I then prayed, asking the Lord to help them find the medal.

The next day I called Mom and she gave me great news. Jim had found the medal in the first box he looked. God does answer prayer, even the ones we may think are insignificant to Him.

Mom agreed to overnight the medal. I waited with anticipation for the mailman. Finally, he arrived with the package that I knew contained the precious cargo. I cut the tape and ripped open the top, anxious yet cautious. There it was, my medal. My Gold medal. It lay at the top, neatly nestled into the special packaging arranged by my mother. I gently slid one hand under the strap and one under the medallion, and lifted it, more like I was picking up a newborn baby than a medal won twenty years ago.

Excitement, elation, and pride all raced through my mind. I almost cried as I remembered all of the time, effort, sweat, and hard work that went into not only my life but the lives of many others in order to achieve this dream. Because of those emotions I knew giving Austin the medal was the perfect way of expressing my thanks for all he had done to help me to hear and win.

Now that I had the medal, just three days before we were to leave, I had to work fast to get it framed and shipped to Minnesota. I took some of the logos and photos from the 1985 yearbook to include in the mounting. I also had a gold plaque made that included the verse: God Loves a Cheerful Giver (2 Cor. 9:7). The frame shop manager said I should sign the letter to be included in the frame. He handed me not a red, black, or blue ink marker, but a gold marker. I thought this was turning out to be beautiful.

The frame shop finished the day before we were to leave. By now, Ginny and I decided it was best to take the framed medal with us instead of shipping it overnight in order to prevent the glass from breaking. We arrived at Orlando International Airport expecting to take the boxed frame on the plane with us. Security personnel had different thoughts. Guards gave us that, "You're kidding, right?" look. A brief discussion ensued. After one of the guards peeked inside the box, we were allowed to carry Austin's rather large framed gift onto the plane.

But we ran into another obstacle when we boarded. A flight attendant told us that because of its size we would have to check the box with the other luggage or mail it. I explained why I didn't want to do either. Two female flight attendants overheard part of the conversation and said we could put it in the back of the plane. Another answered prayer.

Ginny and I arrived in Minnesota late, around 11:00 p.m. A Starkey driver greeted us at baggage claim and wanted to know if we preferred to attend the pre-gala party at Austin's or go straight to the hotel. Of course, I selected the party. I was eager to give him the medal. We pulled up to Austin's house after driving past a line of cars that stretched for what seemed like a mile down the street. I thought this must be some party.

The first person we saw inside was Lou Ferrigno, the bodybuilder who portrayed the Incredible Hulk in the 1970s television show of the same name. He sat on the family room sofa in front of the fireplace reading a magazine. I'd met Lou on numerous occasions before so I jokingly asked if he still worked out.

He replied, "Yeah, I want to look just like you."

I smiled and said, "Keep at it."

We left Lou to get back to his reading and Ginny and I searched throughout the house which was full of people, food and dancing, as well as the Osmond brothers singing on the back porch. Ginny encouraged me to put the medal back in the car and wait until the next day. I didn't want to at first. I was determined, but after looking through the crowd for Austin for some time, I listened to my wife and put the box in the car. We went back inside and finally found Austin entertaining guests in his garage where everyone was having a good time. At first you couldn't tell the room was a garage because of the spotless floor. I think someone could have eaten off it. Then I spotted a Rolls Royce and many other items to be auctioned off at the Gala the next evening.

I hadn't seen Austin in twenty years, yet he greeted us with his signature white hair and familiar big smile. He then introduced us to his guest Michael Bolton and noticed I wore a pair of old Starkey hearing aids.

"What on earth are in your ears?" he said.

I told him, "They're Starkey's, of course."

He said he wanted to see me in his office first thing the next morning. "I have something better that you're going to love." He then graciously escorted Ginny and me on a quick tour of his house. He made us feel welcome and we appreciated his kindness and hospitality.

We stayed at the party until about 1:00 a.m., then retired to a nearby hotel.

The following morning, Justin Osmond came to pick us up for my hearing aid fitting at Starkey headquarters. Before departing the hotel, we showed him Austin's gift. He was excited, smiled and said, "Bill's gonna want to keep this in his bedroom." He called Austin's wife. After a brief conversation they decided it would be best for me to present the medal to Austin during the Gala, if I agreed. I was stunned. All of this was happening because of a simple "thank you" letter inspired by my pastor's sermon a few weeks earlier.

At Starkey, they cleaned the wax from my ears while I watched the process on a monitor. I thought I was watching a scary movie. After my hearing test, Austin fitted my ears with the newest, and much smaller, hearing aids. Austin's energy amazed me, how he could stay up entertaining guests and still arrive at his office first thing in the morning. His passion and enthusiasm for helping people to hear was inspiring, just as it had been twenty years earlier. Watching Austin work encouraged me to give my all on the tennis court while I'm teaching and in the gym while I'm training. His work ethic is contagious.

Ginny and I then spent the better part of the day mingling with the staff and other guests. We enjoyed lunch in the company cafeteria and shared our story of the gold medal I'd give Austin at the Gala that night.

I got my new hearing aids in the course of a few hours. Thanks to Austin's custom fit, they felt as comfortable as a brand new pair of slippers.

That night Ginny and I, dressed in tuxedo and

 evening gown, were driven by shuttle bus to the St. Paul River Center. When we got off the bus, we walked the red carpet with other guests and celebrities.

Inside, the convention center was full of rare and valuable paraphernalia to be auctioned off for the Gala.

To our astonishment, we were given seats at a table in the front of the ballroom. We spent time getting to know everyone at our table while eating. After dinner we were entertained by Yearwood, Bolton, and the Osmonds, then the auction began. Someone tugged at my arm and summoned me backstage. He instructed me to wait for them to call when it was time to give Austin the medal.

Like my engagement to Ginny, I wasn't sure how this presentation was supposed to happen. I waited backstage wondering if somebody would come to get me. Surely they remembered I have to read lips, even with these great hearing aids.

I was about to give away one of my most prized possessions, but remained calm while I waited. A few minutes later the director ran  up to me and asked, "Are you Brad Minns?"

Before I could finish telling him I was, he thrust me on stage. Austin stood at the podium calling my name, waiting for me to come out. I strode across the stage, shook his hand, and turned to face the audience. I couldn't see many faces because of the glare of the bright lights.

 I then told everyone the story of how Bill Austin and Team Starkey had helped not only me, but Team USA and athletes around

the world to receive the gift of hearing. I also shared that Austin's passion for helping others was just as strong twenty years later as it was in 1985. I finished by reading the scripture on the plaque. Then I turned to Austin and said, "Thank you," and gave him the medal.

I learned through this experience it is in our giving that we receive. Luke 6:38 says, "Give, and it will be given to you. A good measure, pressed down, shaken together and running over, will be poured into your lap. For with the measure you use, it will be measured to you."

As a result of being obedient to give away something that meant a lot to me, Ginny and I enjoyed one of the most memorable weekends of our lives, one we certainly won't forget. And we both discovered it is never too late to say "thank you."

"Fear not."

2 Kings 6:16

Chapter 12 | Face Your Fears

While coaching my Christian high school tennis team at a district championship tournament a few years ago, Evan, one of boys' singles players, was getting pummeled by a much more experienced and stronger player. Evan's frustration showed when his opponent won the first set, 6-0. During the changeover, I reminded Evan of the scripture verse "God did not give you a spirit of fear but of courage, love, and a sound mind" (2 Tim. 1:7). At the start of the next set, his demeanor changed. Instead of looking frustrated, discouraged and afraid, he exuded confidence, faith, and belief. Evan won the next two sets and moved onto the next round. At the spring banquet, I shared the story of Evan's victory. I described how oftentimes the difference between winning and losing is where you focus your thoughts.

Are you focused on fear? The fear of not being good enough? The fear of losing? I've learned not to let fear hold me back from going for my dreams. Instead, I face them. It is all a state of mind. If I had given in to the fear of the unknown, I would never have achieved the dreams and goals I set out to do.

When I feel fear, I remind myself that fear is not from God, it's from the enemy. The more I study God's word, the more weapons I have to overcome those fears.

While I worked on this book with my wife, I often feared it might not be good enough. When those thoughts surfaced, I reminded myself to keep pressing forward one day at a time and finish. I believe God put this dream on my heart to encourage, bless and help others, so I pressed on and trusted God.

Public speaking is one thing that terrified me. This shouldn't come as a big surprise. Polls consistently show public speaking is people's number one fear. Most of those polled can probably hear. So imagine my fear.

The first time I spoke in front of an audience occurred at my high school's spring sports banquet in 1983. The tennis team captain asked me at the last minute to receive the Great Lakes league championship trophy. This meant I had to go up in front of the athletic boosters, other teams, parents, teachers, and students to give a speech. I thought, he couldn't be serious, but he was. He must have known that I struggled at times to pronounce a select number of words. My body temperature rose, my head spun, and my palms began to sweat. Suddenly, the spaghetti on my plate didn't interest me.

When it came time, I walked onto the stage, accepted the award, shook the presenter's hand, proceeded to a microphone and gave the best ten-second speech ... that no one heard. After a quick glimpse of the engraving on the award, I looked up to see a cafeteria full of people staring at me. Before I could wonder why, the emcee guided me to the other microphone, one that was turned "on." I smiled and, red-faced, repeated my lines, "On behalf of the boys' varsity tennis team, I would like to thank all of you for making this season possible." That was it. In what seemed like the worst event of my life up to that point, I had given a speech I was totally unprepared for.

Despite the high-fives and hugs from my teammates, I vowed to never speak publicly again. God obviously had other plans.

Soon after winning the World Games for the Deaf in Los Angeles, I was named the 1985 Providence Speech and Hearing Center's Athlete Citizen of the year. My brother Jim and I were flown to Palm Springs, California, for the event and we met many celebrities: Chad Everett, Beau Bridges, Alan Hale Jr. (the skipper from *Gilligan's Island*), and Barry Williams from *The Brady Bunch*, to name a few.

The day of the awards ceremony, a limousine picked up Jim and me at our hotel. Los Angeles Rams cheerleaders greeted us when we arrived at the resort. Jim and I smiled at each other and thought, wow, this is great.

But the euphoria soon went away when I learned at dinner that I had to give an acceptance speech. Again, the butterflies, sweaty palms, and fear consumed my thoughts. I was about to speak in front of professional athletes, celebrities, umpires, and beautiful cheerleaders. During my speech I thanked Jim for being a great coach and brother. Without him I wouldn't be the tennis player I was. I thanked Jim and everyone else involved in giving me the award. I felt relieved when it was over and vowed to never give another public speech again.

Jim and I had a great time that night and the next day participating in the Lloyd Bridges celebrity tennis event sponsored by the Starkey Hearing Foundation, sitting by the pool, and listening to Everett crack jokes whenever we saw him. At the weekend's golf event, Jim finished among the leaders.

When we got back to Toledo, before I had a chance to unpack, my tennis coach approached me at practice and said, "Congratulations, Brad. You've been chosen the University of Toledo's Scholar Athlete of the Year."

I said "What for? How can I get the scholar athlete with my grades?"

"I don't know, but Jim Harbaugh is going to present it to you."

"You're kidding right?"

Coach said, "Nope."

"Do I have to give a speech?"

Coach said, "Yep."

"Great," I said with a hint of sarcasm.

The award, sponsored by the Cystic Fibrosis Foundation, is presented each year to an athlete for

outstanding athletic and academic achievement. Jim Harbaugh, now coach of the National Football League San Francisco 49ers, was scheduled to present the award. At the time, Harbaugh was the standout quarterback for the University of Michigan. Again, I remember being nervous that night. My dad, brother, and a cousin attended with me and did their best to boost my confidence. Most of the time I couldn't hear what anybody said because of the background noise. And I didn't hear any of Harbaugh's twenty-minute speech. I sat in a chair behind him, but I could see people laughing at his stories.

When Harbaugh finished, the emcee handed me the microphone. Oh boy, I thought and did my best to  pronounce Cystic Fibrosis. I don't remember what I said when Harbaugh presented me with the award. I do remember looking out over the audience full of distinguished guests who had given their hard-earned money to make the event possible and wondering how on earth I had been selected to receive this prestigious award.

In a small way, I can understand how Moses must have felt when God told him to go to the Pharaoh and tell him to let His people go. Moses didn't want to go because he had a stuttering problem and was afraid, saying "Who am I, please send someone else."

If someone told me twenty years ago that I'd speak at churches and schools about how God turned my life around, I wouldn't have believed it. Today, by the grace of God, I'm no longer afraid of public speaking. I am thankful for any opportunity to share my testimony with others.

One summer, I was invited to be a guest speaker at a Fellowship of Christian Athletes boy's summer camp in Black Mountain, North Carolina. The Dean, a burly fellow who the boys respected, sat beside Ginny and me as I waited to give my speech. The Dean got up and made his way to the microphone. He motioned for the boys to be seated. The boys sat in unison. Then he introduced me by saying, "Our next speaker came all the way from Orlando. He is the former world *blind* tennis champion. Please welcome him."

As the Dean left the stage and the boys politely clapped, Ginny nudged me in the arm and said, "Brad he just introduced you as the former world 'blind' tennis champion."

Walking to the stage, I realized he was right. I am a former "blind" tennis champion. When I made it to the microphone, I told the audience I was the former world's *deaf* tennis champion, but the Dean was correct in his introduction. I once was blind but now I see. Everyone laughed.

I thank God for his amazing grace. Grace means unmerited favor. Grace is God's goodness, His gift.

Ephesians 2:8 says, "We are saved by grace and not by works lest anyone should boast." Grace is a gift that must be received by faith.

"Amazing Grace" is a beautiful song that I heard quite often as a youth. I never understood the words though until I became a believer in Jesus Christ.

Whenever I was afraid to do something, after facing it, I felt stronger. That may include speaking in public, beginning an exercise program, sharing your faith, going back to school, or whatever else it may be in your life.

I'm blessed because of what Jesus Christ has done in my life and I love sharing that with others, wherever and whenever the Holy Spirit leads me.

I learned a long time ago that fear can keep us from fulfilling our God-given purpose, if we give in to it. Overcoming fear takes courage. We can rely on Jesus and live out Psalm 31:24, which says, "Be strong and take heart, all you who hope in the Lord."

Today, I get excited about speaking to others and encouraging people not to give up on their God-given dreams. I count it an honor and a privilege. This confidence doesn't come from self, but from Christ within. It comes from knowing who I am in Christ. It's Christ confidence that gives me the ability to face fears head on and overcome them. The same can be true for you too.

I believe God gives each of us everything we need to accomplish His will for our lives. For me, God gave me a supportive family whose patience and sacrifice helped me learn how to communicate so I can enjoy teaching tennis and fitness. I am also blessed to be able to share God's word and do my best to lead a healthy, fit lifestyle to be a good example for the upcoming generation.

Looking through the windshield of life rather than the rear view mirror, gives you a clearer vision for the future. If we look through the rear view mirror, it's difficult to see where we're going. I'm proud of my past accomplishments on and off the tennis court, but nothing compares to the future God has for me or anyone else who puts their trust in Him. God promises us this in His word, "What no eye has seen, what no ear has heard, and what no human mind has conceived, the things God has prepared for those who love him" (1 Cor. 2:9).

I want to encourage you to go for your dreams and never give up. With God all things are possible. Keep pressing forward in life. Whatever dream God has placed in your heart, trust Him and go forward. Courage isn't the absence of fear, it's moving forward past the fear. Fear tries to torment you, but faith in God will deliver you.

I learned not to let fear hold me back from going for my dreams. Instead, I face them. It is all a state of mind. If I had given in to the fear of the unknown, I would never have achieved the dreams and goals I set out to do.

What dream has God given you? What are you afraid of? Pray, and ask God to help you face whatever fear that tries to keep you from God's best. Each time you take a step of faith, your faith grows stronger.

If you don't step out of your comfort zone, you will remain where you are. If you refuse to take any kind of action, nothing will get accomplished.

"Strengthen your feeble arms and weak knees."
Hebrews 12:12

Chapter 13 | Invest in Your Health

A 1970s "Keep America Beautiful" television commercial featured a Native American rowing in a canoe past a factory dumping waste in a river, walking through trash on the shore, and then standing along a highway while a passenger threw trash that landed at his feet. The camera zoomed in on the Indian's face as the announcer said,

"People can start pollution; people can stop it." A tear rolled down his cheek. The message of the public service announcement was simple: We must be responsible for our actions and think about how they can affect others, whether in a positive or a negative way.

Some of the basic principles I've learned over the years to incorporate in my personal life are prayer, exercise and proper nutrition.

As a personal trainer I've seen some people achieve their goals quicker than others. Some give up too soon because they aren't seeing the results they want right away. These people haven't learned to persevere. But for those who decide to stay committed to their program, eventually their lives change for the better. We don't lose our health and fitness overnight, and we can't get it back overnight either. The habits we develop can either make us or break us. We must learn to develop great habits if we are to live our best life.

Ask any financial planner and they will encourage you to invest for the long-term. This means never spending more than you earn and setting aside a little bit each month for saving and investing. When applied consistently, this strategy can enable one to become financially stronger. At first, these modest deposits don't seem like much. But over time, the power of compounding kicks in and these small deposits begin to pay large dividends.

The same is true of exercise. I began making deposits toward my physical fitness many years ago. I can confess with confidence it's a great way to live. Since I began my long-term investment program in physical fitness, I have strengthened my body, which has improved my tennis, confidence and overall outlook on life. Fitness can do the same for you. Commit yourself today to start making daily deposits to your health. I am confident that given time, your small deposits of healthy eating and exercise will pay great dividends.

Lifting weights will improve muscular strength and increase fat loss. For those who don't have much time to invest in their exercise program, studies show one good set of a particular exercise is 95-percent as effective as doing four or five sets. This means you get the same results in less than half the time. So, there are no more excuses for not having enough time in the day. If you have twenty minutes three times a week for weight training, that should be plenty.

The most important deposit you can make is in the area of nutrition. Start eating foods that build muscle, increase energy levels, and make you feel vibrant.

The late Jack LaLanne, considered by many the first fitness guru, said it best, "Exercise is king, nutrition is

queen, put them together and you've got a kingdom." He also said, "If man made it, don't eat it."

Moderation is the key. Make water the beverage of choice. I prefer sparkling mineral water with a little bit of my favorite juice added. This allows me to keep my calories lower and yet have a cool, tasty beverage. When Ginny and I go shopping, we make it a point to read the labels. If we can't pronounce the ingredients, we usually don't buy it. We start at the outer perimeter where there are fresh fruits and vegetables, eggs, and lean meats. We buy few items from the center aisles of the store where we get our oats, olive oil, peanut butter, nuts and seeds. Most items in the center aisles are processed foods.

Each of us is responsible to do our part and care for the bodies we have been blessed to receive. When we're committed, it becomes a lifestyle like no other. Being fit, healthy and strong isn't a short term goal; it's a way of life.

Below are some of the exercises I've used over the years to help build my physique. If applied consistently, they can do the same for you. They are basic bodybuilding exercises to lay the foundation for your physical fitness. When living a healthy lifestyle, you will feel stronger, have more energy, more optimism, and enjoy a better overall outlook on your life.

Daily:
- Sixty-minute walk (can be broken up throughout the day in fifteen-minute increments)
- Read the Bible
- Pray

Suggested Workout: For Abs exercises, perform 50-100 of each. All other exercises, perform 1-3 sets of 8-15 reps. Use weights you are able to lift with proper form, then increase as you get stronger while achieving the desired amount of reps.

My favorite Abs routine:

Bar twist
Crunch
Reverse crunch
Bicycle crunch
Side oblique crunch
Superman

Monday:
(Chest, Shoulders, Triceps)

Bench press
Inclines bench press
Dumbbell flys
Side laterals
Dumbbell upright rows
Front raises
Dumbbell extensions
Bench dips
Rope push downs

Tuesday: Running and tennis-
(20-30 minutes of Cardio)   specific training

Wednesday: Wide-grip pull downs
(Back and Biceps)   One-arm dumbbell rows
                                      Straight-arm pull downs
                                      Dead lifts
                                      Hammer Curls
                                      Cable curls

Thursday: High-intensity running
(20-30 minutes of Cardio)   and/or
                                      tennis-specific training

Friday: Leg extensions
(Legs and Calves)   Barbell squats
                                      Dumbbell lunges (each leg)
                                      Standing leg curls
                                      (each leg)
                                      One-leg Romanian dead
                                      lift (each leg)
                                      Glute bridge
                                      Standing calf raises
                                      Seated calf press

Everyday: After the workout, make
                                      time to stretch

<u>Nutrition Tips:</u>

- Eat five to six small meals a day.
- Drink eight 8-ounce glasses of water a day. Choose all-natural foods, such as fresh fruits and vegetables. You will spend more money on the food, but in the long run you will save money because you'll have better health.
- Shop the outer aisles at the grocery store and look for the items listed below.
- Store ready-to-drink protein shakes in the fridge for those with limited time.
- Brad's nutrition protein shake recipe: two scoops of whey protein, one cup of water, one teaspoon of peanut butter, whole banana, one teaspoon of dark chocolate cocoa powder, two teaspoons of glutamine and crushed ice to taste.
- Choose quality proteins, such as chicken, turkey, lean beef, and eggs.
- Snack on healthy nuts such as walnuts, almonds, pecans, and macadamias.

Fitness Tips:

- Consult your physician before embarking on any exercise program.
- Set realistic weekly, monthly, and yearly goals and adjust accordingly.
- Keep a workout journal to monitor your progress.
- Commit to the fitness lifestyle, not a temporary get fit quick routine.
- Exercise daily. Run, bike, play tennis—whatever it is you like—until you break a sweat.
- Visualize yourself being active, healthy and happy.
- Read exercise books and magazines so you can be inspired daily.
- Get at least a day or two of rest in between training each body part to provide adequate recovery and avoid overtraining.
- Persevere and don't give up on your dream.

"Run in such a way as to get the prize."
1 Corinthians 9:24

Chapter 14 | What Race Are You Running?

"Run, come on, run." My brother Jim turned and yelled to motivate me to keep up with him as we jogged around the neighborhood block. Jim wanted to sprint home and finish strong. I was about thirteen at the time and knew Jim was right, but I didn't want to run. I was lazy and my brother knew he had to push me to do more. After his encouragement fell on deaf ears (pun intended), he grabbed my shirt and pulled me along. I still barely had the energy or motivation to jog back to the house where I would have rather been on the sofa watching television.

Later in life I discovered we're in a race—every day. And what we do each day matters. 1 Corinthians 9:24 says, "Do you not know that in a race all the runners run, but only one gets the prize? Run in such a way as to get the prize." We have the choice of which race to run: the world's race or God's race. Early in life I ran in the world's race trying to get ahead and prove myself according to the world's standards. Now I run God's race with joy, hope, and confidence. Spending a few moments each morning in a quiet place reading the bible, and praying gives me a sense of spiritual well-being and a closer walk with the Lord. I also make it a point to read good books throughout the day to reinforce my beliefs. There is a lot of negativity in the world and negative people. To keep from becoming negative I practice being positive each day. I do this by spending time with the Lord and meditating on his word throughout the day.

While I enjoy playing tennis and lifting weights more than ever, my passion is teaching others life lessons, such as the importance of commitment, dedication and perseverance. I also get satisfaction from telling others about how God has turned my life around. Early in our marriage, Jimmy, a young resident in the apartment complex where we lived, came to the weekly tennis lessons at the complex. And he sometimes hung out in the apartment gym and often asked me for fitness tips and how he could build muscle. He showed a lot of interest in body building. I lost touch with Jimmy after Ginny and I moved into our first home in September 2006.

One day while I worked out at a local gym near our home, Jimmy, now a college student, approached me. I didn't recognize him at first because he was much bigger. He gave me a bear hug and said how much I'd inspired him to lift weights. His dream then was to become a personal trainer like myself so he too could encourage others. That day in the gym I shared what God had done in my life. I told him how God transformed me and how He saved me from my sins. I explained how I received forgiveness from my sins by receiving Jesus into my heart. It was the first time I shared my faith with Jimmy and I could tell by his reaction that God was speaking to him. I never saw Jimmy again. Several weeks later, his mother sent me an email saying that Jimmy had unexpectedly passed away. She was distraught over her loss, but told me about the influence I had been in Jimmy's life, and for that she was thankful. Her email inspired me to be more of a hopeful influence to others.

Looking back, that day in the gym was a divine appointment. God knows all of our days, and He is always trying to speak to us. However, it's our decision whether we listen to Him or not. We also have a free will to receive what He is trying to say to us. I believe Jimmy heard God that day and is now living with Him in paradise.

Weightlifting, tennis, or anything else won't save a person. Only Jesus does. That's why I am passionate about sharing Him with others. James 4:14 says, "Yet you do not know what your life will be like tomorrow. You are just a vapor that appears for a little while and then vanishes away."

This is what motivates me to get up in the morning. To live my life not for myself but for Jesus and to do His will. God didn't send His Son to judge the world. He sent Him to save it.

In my journey, I have discovered it's not how we start, it's how we finish. The first thirty years of my life, I pursued and achieved a lot of my goals and dreams. Proverbs 14:12 says, "There is a way that appears to be right, but in the end it leads to death."

I thought I knew what was right. But I didn't. When I looked around at the rest of the world, I thought I was on the right road. I discovered I was spiritually bankrupt. After spending the first part of my life building the outer man, I was dead inside. While building my outer man, I neglected my inner spirit man.

The following story is a good example of running the wrong way. On October 25, 1964, Minnesota's Jim Marshall picked up a fumble by the San Francisco receiver and ran toward the end zone. The 49ers home crowd roared as Marshall lumbered down the middle of the field. He may have thought the fans were cheering him on and he ran sixty-six yards untouched into the end zone. After he crossed the goal line, Marshall tossed the ball out of bounds and turned to walk back to the bench. While the crowd continued to roar, a Niners offensive lineman met Marshall at the five-yard-line and told him that he had run into the wrong end zone. Marshall hung his head. Years later, the play was ranked first in NFL Film's 100 Greatest Follies.

Running in the right direction—toward God—involves more than attending church once a week or during holidays. Each morning before anything else, give God the first part of your day by reading His word and talking to Him in prayer. Get involved in a Bible study and fellowship with other believers. Joshua 1:8 says, "Do not let this Book of the Law depart from your mouth; meditate on it day and night, so that you may be careful to do everything written in it. Then you will be prosperous and successful."

Know that God loves you and wants what is best for you. He is on your side. He created you for a purpose. Trust Him with your life. I encourage you to get to know Him, allow Him to speak into your life, and guide you with His wisdom. When you surrender your life to Jesus Christ you will know the joy and peace which passes all understanding.

I pray the lessons I've learned and written about in this book will inspire you to live your life to the fullest, to be all you were created to be, and to receive everything good God has planned for you.

If you haven't yet made Jesus Christ the Lord of your life, I encourage you to do it today. Tomorrow may be too late. Realize you need a savior and pray the salvation prayer below. Romans 10:9 says, "That if you confess with your mouth, 'Jesus is Lord' and believe in your heart that God raised him from the dead, you will be saved."

Salvation Prayer to receive Jesus Christ as your Lord and Savior:

Dear God,

I know that I am a sinner and need Your forgiveness. I believe that Jesus Christ died for my sins. I am willing to turn from my sins. I now invite Jesus Christ to come into my heart and life as my personal Savior. I am willing, by God's strength, to follow and obey Jesus Christ as the Lord of my life.

Thank You Lord,
Amen.

The Author

Brad was born in Toledo Ohio on June 9, 1965. At the age of three he lost his hearing when he contracted a deadly fever. Rather than send him to special schools, his parents made sure Brad knew how to read lips and had him fitted with hearing aids.

He began playing sports and found that he had an interest in tennis, which he began to participate in more and more. He went on to become one of the top junior players in his age division and received a scholarship at the University of Toledo as a walk on. The only difference between Brad and his teammates was the fact that he couldn't hear the cheers of the crowds who came to watch him play. After college he went on to become the USA's number one deaf tennis player and won numerous World Deaf Championships. He also helped the USA to win its first ever Dresse Cup in 1995.

Not being content with just playing professional tennis at the World level, he began using his bodybuilding in earnest. In 1995 he won the P.A.S./Experimental and Applied Sciences nutritional supplement transformation contest now known as Body-for-Life and became their second national spokesperson.

In addition to being the E.A.S. second spokesman, his bodybuilding success earned him various modeling jobs including being Nordic Flex's cover model and appeared in their National television advertising campaign.

Brad has always met his goals and is now determined to teach others how to go for their dreams and goals. Today, Brad lives with his wife Ginny in Orlando, FL and works as a tennis professional and personal trainer. He speaks at FCA (Fellowship of Christian Athletes) groups where he shares his testimony of living a life for Christ.

NEVER GIVE UP

To contact Brad or to request additional information:

E-mail: Brad@bradminns.com

or visit Brad's website at:

www.bradminns.com